Christ's
Radiant
Church

John Hosier

MonarcH
BOOKS

Oxford, UK & Grand Rapids, Michigan, USA

First published in the UK in 2005 by Monarch Books
(a publishing imprint of Lion Hudson plc),
Mayfield House, 256 Banbury Road, Oxford OX2 7DH.
Tel: +44 (0) 1865 302750   Fax: +44 (0) 1865 302757
Email: monarch@lionhudson.com
www.lionhudson.com

ISBN 1 85424 700 X (UK)
ISBN 0 8254 6088 3 (USA)

Distributed by:
UK: Marston Book Services Ltd, PO Box 269,
Abingdon, Oxon OX14 4YN;
USA: Kregel Publications, PO Box 2607,
Grand Rapids, Michigan 49501.

British Library Cataloguing Data
A catalogue record for this book is available
from the British Library.

Book design and production for the publishers by Lion Hudson plc.
Printed in Great Britain.

Contents

Foreword

Coming from a non-Christian background, I was amazed when I was told that I could know God personally. God had always seemed a distant and remote being. After some lengthy conversation I accepted Jesus as my personal Saviour and began to develop my personal devotions and tried falteringly to get involved in personal evangelism.

Finding a 'church of my choice' was regarded as somewhat secondary. Getting right with God was clearly regarded as the main thing, and being assured of my own personal destiny was all important.

Indeed, at the time of my conversion Christians seemed to be not very enthusiastic about the Church. Rather apologetically, they advised the new Christian not to look at the Church but to look at Jesus. The Church was something of an embarrassment.

This attitude hardly reflected the Biblical perspective where the Church is seen as fundamental to God's glorious purpose in the earth. Jesus confidently and purposefully announced, 'I will build my church.' He was preoccupied with gathering a people for Himself. Undoubtedly, it could be argued that God's chief desire in the creation of man was to have a people for Himself of whom He could say, 'I am theirs and they are mine.' No theme of Scripture so reveals God's ultimate goal than the oft repeated, 'I will be to them a God and they will be to me a people.' The whole story concludes with the climax of the Church, brilliant with the glory of God, made ready as a bride adorned for her husband. She is his ultimate goal and passion.

When Christians, therefore, are indifferent or even embarrassed about the Church, they have thoroughly failed to reflect Christ's preoccupation.

He is determined to have a spotless bride that has made herself ready for the marriage of the Lamb. You may be tempted to reply, 'This is the universal church that no man can number, not our experience of a local congregation.' Undoubtedly this would be His primary focus but should we, therefore, expect the local assembly to be in such contrast to God's grand design? Paul wrote to the church at Corinth saying that he wanted to present them as a pure virgin to Christ. The local congregation reflects God's ultimate goal for His whole church.

The book of Revelation shows Jesus, not as one vaguely in the midst of the church, but as one who walks among the individual lampstands. He knows each intimately, commending one and warning another. He applauds steadfastness here and challenges apathy there. Each is an open book to Him and His longing for a glorious bride is evident in His concern and ambition for each particular congregation.

Paul did not simply work to win converts but to plant churches. He did not regard his evangelising work as complete until elders had been appointed and churches formed. It was through the establishing of local churches that the kingdom of God was to be extended. 'Being added' was the definitive expression that Luke used to describe the conversion of thousands in the early chapters of Acts.

Believers need to rediscover a passion for the Church. We need to see its centrality in God's purpose. We need to understand how essential it is for the individual to be meaningfully joined to a body of believers where his or her sanctification can be outworked in the context of spiritual partnership. It is impossible for the lone Christian to reach maturity. Only in close proximity with other believers can we learn to overcome the challenges of selfishness, immaturity and ungodliness.

Only in the context of vibrant local church life can we

embrace the full impact of the presence of the Holy Spirit. He comes to indwell a body, to fill a temple, to fortify an army.

God has made us interdependent people, reconciled by His love beyond the barriers of race, gender, wealth, tribe and tongue. The Church is a glorious display and demonstration of Christ's magnificent power to reconcile the apparently irreconcilable and unite as one. Only Jesus can do it! Only He can bring about the harmony from such divergent people that brings glory to God.

For churches to be brought to such maturity requires the restoration of much that has been lost. In this volume, John Hosier brings to the reader's attention many areas of church life in profound need of recovery to Biblical norms. He has covered a wide variety of subjects from marriage to mission, from worship to women, from family to flexibility. He demonstrates painstaking submission to the text of Scripture and repeatedly illustrates from personal experience of local church life.

The book in your hands comes to you with the urgent desire that God will stir your motivation to recover authentic church life, leading to a corporate maturity and a brilliant testimony to the world of what the people of God should truly be, Christ's radiant Church.

Terry Virgo
13th April 2005

Introduction

I have spent almost my entire working life in full-time leadership in local churches. I love the local church and although I sometimes speak at Christian conferences I am happiest when I have the opportunity to serve an individual church.

I have often heard it said, and I agree, that the church is God's plan A to evangelise the world and there is no plan B. If this is true then it is vital that we plant and establish churches according to the biblical pattern.

Every denomination and every church movement has probably, at times, been guilty of the pride of thinking that their way of doing church is the correct way. One of the problems with this, is that God sometimes seems to bless others more than us, even those apparently not building correctly! Nevertheless reforming and renewal movements of church life have surfaced again and again in history.

In the second half of the twentieth century and into the twenty-first century there has grown up what have variously been referred to as House Churches, Restoration Churches, or New Churches. This has been seen in the planting of many new local churches, the transformation of numbers of older local churches and has also presented a challenge to many established churches. Certainly there has been a passion to get back to the kind of church life about which we read in the New Testament. The story circulates of someone who once criticised Billy Graham for trying to take the church back 100 years by his evangelistic style and preaching. Billy responded by saying that he was rather disappointed as he hoped to take it back

9

2000 years! The New Churches also share that desire, but at the same time want to be absolutely relevant to the present age.

Because the New Churches have emphasised the person and work of the Holy Spirit they are known to be charismatic and generally would be viewed as belonging to the more Pentecostal wing of the universal church. They would also be regarded often as theologically shallow – strong on the Spirit and weak on the Word. Many of us would protest we are strong on the Spirit precisely because we are strong on the Word.

This book, therefore, is about biblical values. It is not the story of one particular local church, although a lot of the illustrations are drawn from the local church to which I belong.

Within the Newfrontiers group of churches of which I am a member, I have often heard it said that we do not have our key biblical convictions all laid out in one book. I hope I have made some contribution to addressing that need.

But more generally this book is intended to help other parts of the body of Christ understand the biblical convictions of the New Churches and therefore, hopefully, to offer a contribution, more widely, to the restoration of the church today.

Chapter 1   # Restoration
God's ultimate purpose

Events occur that remind us of the swift passing of time and the briefness of our existence on this earth. A celebration of my parents' golden wedding brought back memories of their silver wedding as though it was only yesterday! James asks: 'What is your life? You are a mist that appears for a little while and then vanishes' (James 4:14).

We have a temporary residence on the earth, but we have a permanent residence in what the apostle Paul calls the heavenly realm – a citizenship in heaven. Paul tells us that it is our union with Christ that gives us this permanency of residence and we can enjoy every spiritual blessing in the heavenly realm. This is the revelatory teaching given in the first half of Ephesians 1, which must rank with Romans 8 as one of the most profound chapters in the Bible.

It is encouraging to remind ourselves of these spiritual blessings for they are really of more importance to us than anything we can know or possess in the present earthly realm. We tend, especially in the West, to get thrilled by material blessings in the earthly realm, but these are only transient. An unexpected tax return is what can really excite us. But our spiritual blessings in the heavenly realm are what really count, for they are not only real now, but also forever.

The spiritual blessings that Paul lists in Ephesians 1 can be very practically applied. If we lack a job then we can feel that no one wants us. But Paul tells us that God wants us, for he has chosen us even before creation began. We may have a very difficult family situation, but Paul reminds us that we have been predestined to be the adopted sons of God. We may have really messed up our life in the past; but we have now been redeemed through the blood of Christ.

It is wonderful to be united to Christ, or to use Paul's favourite phrase, to be 'in Christ' with all the riches of God's grace being lavished on us.

The end of the world

Another of the great spiritual blessings mentioned in Ephesians 1 that follows from our being 'in Christ' is that we are given insight into the secrets of God.

> *And he made known to us the mystery of his will according to his good pleasure, which he purposed in Christ, to be put into effect when the times will have reached their fulfilment – to bring all things in heaven and on earth together under one head, even Christ (Ephesians 1:9–10).*

We are never short of prophecies pointing to some disastrous event that will bring an end to the world. Some believe that we are going to be hit by a meteor from space that will finish us off. The problems created by the population explosion have led others to speculate that 2050 AD is about the possible limit of our survival. Those born before, during, or shortly after the Second World War grew up very conscious of the nuclear threat to the world during the dark days of the 'cold war'. Even now some rogue state might develop nuclear weapons, the use of which could threaten the world's very existence.

Religious people have certainly not been shy in suggesting dates for the end of the world. The Jehovah's Witnesses have lost all credibility, except among their own members, for several suggestions of dates for the consummation of history, all of which have now passed! A few years back a book was published in the USA giving 88 reasons why the Rapture of the church would probably occur in 1988. However, you may have noticed that the church is still here!

In Ephesians 1 there is truth about the end of the world and the end of this age that is now being revealed to us. Paul tells us that God has made known to us the mystery of his will and that this is to be put into effect when the times have reached their fulfilment, that is at the end of the age.

When Paul speaks of the mystery of God's will he is not talking about something odd or peculiar, but something previously kept secret, but now revealed. This is one of our spiritual blessings, for God has made known to us who are 'in Christ', his will for the end of the age.

Paul begins Ephesians 1 by telling us that God was choosing his people in eternity, even before creation. Then Paul covers other spiritual blessings before he sweeps on to inform us about the very end of history when the times will have reached their fulfilment. History is moving towards a climax, and one with a very clear goal. God has an amazing purpose for history and creation. God has chosen to reveal to us who are 'in Christ' what that purpose is.

We should feel the drama of this revelation. It is easy to read verses in Ephesians 1 scores of times and for them to become very familiar, and then for us to be dulled to the truth by that very familiarity. In fact there is a most amazing disclosure. We are the people of God; we are those who are 'in Christ'. Paul has been unfolding the details of what this means by enumerating our spiritual blessings. Now God reveals to us his ultimate purpose and final plan, which is: 'to bring all things in heaven and on earth together under one head, even Christ' (Ephesians 1:10). It is not just a nice comment; it is a phenomenal revelation. God has told us what he is going to do at the end of history.

Some years ago I was involved in helping to arrange an evangelistic crusade that lasted for nearly three weeks. The preacher was a very effective communicator and many responded to the gospel appeal each evening. Listening to his message night after night, I felt that his preaching on the

Second Coming of Christ was probably the most powerful of his evangelistic sermons. The message came across with increased dramatic force due to a tremendous thunderstorm over the tent in which we were sitting! Yet, that night fewer people responded to the appeal than on any previous evening. I was genuinely surprised. Talking to the evangelist afterwards he said that this was his common experience. He believed that during a three-week crusade it was important for him to preach on the Second Coming as part of the presentation of the whole gospel. But he wondered if the concepts were so big that people could not get their mind around them.

That could be true for us as we read Ephesians 1:9 and 10. There is such mighty truth here, but it may be such a huge concept that our mind fails to get hold of what we are reading. Here, in fact, is a dramatic revelation to those 'in Christ'. God's purpose and plan is ultimately to deal with the whole universe, as all things in heaven and earth will be brought together under the headship of Jesus Christ.

Other scriptures

There are other scriptures that tell us the same truth.

> *For God was pleased to have all his fulness dwell in him, (Christ), and through him to reconcile to himself all things, whether things on earth or things in heaven, by making peace through his blood, shed on the cross (Colossians 1:19–20).*

'Reconciled' has the same force as: 'to bring all things ... together' in Ephesians 1. But in Colossians 1 Paul adds that this reconciliation will be accomplished through Christ's blood. Christ's death, with the shedding of his blood, does not only redeem people from their sins and reconcile them to God, but will be finally effective to reconcile the whole created universe to himself.

The 'all things' spoken of in both Ephesians and Colossians

is the term the Bible uses to refer to the whole of creation: the heavens and the earth. All creation has been affected by the fall resulting from sin. Genesis makes it clear that the fall caused havoc not only for mankind but for all that God made as well (see Genesis 3:17).

The effectiveness of Christ's shed blood, and therefore his death, is seen in that it is powerful enough finally to redeem the whole universe and reunite it in perfect harmony under the headship of Jesus Christ.

In Romans 8 we read:

> *The creation waits in eager expectation for the sons of God to be revealed. For the creation was subjected to frustration, not by its own choice, but by the will of the one who subjected it, in hope that the creation itself will be liberated from its bondage to decay and brought into the glorious freedom of the children of God (vv. 19–21).*

God predestined us to be his sons. However in this earthly realm that is not seen and understood. Unbelievers may know that we are Christians, but they do not recognise us as children of God with the full rights of sonship! We alone know that is what we are and what we have. When Jesus returns, the sons of God, and that means every believer, will be revealed, and everyone will see who we really are. Creation itself is waiting for that day, which will coincide with its own liberation, and it will come at the consummation of the ages.

On the same 'day' as the sons of God are revealed creation itself will be set free from all frustration and decay. These days we are all 'green' enough to know the general facts about over-usage of the world's resources, pollution, deforestation, and so on ... God's ultimate plan is not to leave creation to grow ever more frustrated, but to restore the whole of creation to perfection under the headship of Jesus. 'All things' will be reconciled to Christ because of his shed blood.

The full power of that blood will be shown on the day that

this age ends, when Christ returns and even creation, at present so polluted, ravaged and in decay, will be set free from every limitation.

Again we see this in 2 Peter 3:12,13:

> ... *That day will bring about the destruction of the heavens by fire, and the elements will melt in the heat. But in keeping with his promise we are looking forward to a new heaven and a new earth, the home of righteousness.*

Creation is not simply going to rot away with the earth left to disintegrate, a dying planet in a collapsing universe. God has a plan for what he has made. It is a plan for life, liberty, renewal and restoration – a new heaven and a new earth filled only with God's righteousness.

Right through the Bible

This coming renewal of creation is the consistent teaching of the Bible.

Isaiah prophesies it when speaking for the Lord: 'Behold I will create new heavens and a new earth' (Isaiah 65:17).

Jesus teaches on this in the gospels. He said: 'I tell you the truth, at the renewal of all things, when the Son of Man sits on his glorious throne ... ' (Matthew 19:28).

It is the same promise that can be found in the earliest preaching of the apostles: 'He must remain in heaven until the time comes for God to restore everything, as he promised long ago through his holy prophets' (Acts 3:21).

When we come to the Book of Revelation, John informs us that prophecy has been fulfilled as he sees the outworking of God's ultimate plan. 'Then I saw a new heaven and a new earth ... ' (Revelation 21:1). John is declaring that all that the prophets and the scriptures testify to is true; that finally there is a new heaven and earth; everything is made new.

This blessing of the Holy Spirit given to those of us 'in

Christ' is revelation about such a tumultuous event that it can be hard to appreciate fully what is being made known to us. God has unveiled to us his secret purpose; something that is unknown to unbelievers. Christ will be King forever over a new heaven and earth filled only with righteousness.

In a word, God's ultimate plan is *Restoration*. He is going to restore the whole of his creation. This is revealed to us who are 'in Christ'. We have been brought in on the secret, for every blessing of the Holy Spirit is ours in the heavenly realm.

The church

In the light of these blessings, but most particularly because God's ultimate plan is to restore all things, we must highlight the position of the church. We could ask where does the church get a mention in Ephesians 1:3–10?

There is a story of the Baptist pastor who was so committed to his doctrine on baptism that no matter what subject he was preaching on he would always conclude with: 'And finally a few words about water baptism'! So, finally, on the theme of every spiritual blessing being ours, we come to a few words about the church! But where does that really fit in?

We have a theme in Ephesians 1 to motivate the church. Many local churches today are working hard to see a restoration to that which is genuinely biblical in the body of Christ. This is the reason that so many new church movements like Newfrontiers have been spawned in the past few decades. Over the years there have been teachings in the Bible, relevant to the church, that have got left out of church life, for example, spiritual gifts. Other things not in the Bible have sometimes crept into the church. The New Testament doesn't teach us to prioritise buildings, let alone call the buildings 'church', nor does it teach us that leaders should wear special and peculiar clothes! This book will touch on a number of other examples.

To have a vision to restore the church to its true biblical expression is a great motivation.

But there is another aspect to that motivation, in that God will finally restore all things under the headship of Christ. The church, presently in the earthly realm, will be caught up in that final restoration. For it is the church that will live in the new creation. To seek to restore the church now to the Bible's description of how the church should be, surely reflects God's heart for the final restoration of all things under Christ.

Although the local church is based in the earthly realm we can actually view it as an outpost of heaven. There is a colony of heaven based here on the earth. The dream is for each church to be like heaven on earth!

In Roman times colonies were established in different parts of the Empire by settling retired soldiers there. These colonies sought to replicate Rome in the way that justice was administered, social customs were followed and life in general was carried on in a very Roman style. In a Roman colony you could almost have been in Rome itself.

How about being involved in seeking to build a church that looks like heaven; so like heaven that you could almost be there! That is not easy when the history of the church would suggest there has often been more commitment to disintegration or separation than restoration. We have an enemy who wants the church to be torn apart, who wants to break up leadership teams and smash relationships. To see a biblically restored church involves hard work, but God's passion for restoration should stir our own passion for this.

As we remind ourselves in the light of Ephesians 1 of the descriptions of our spiritual blessings 'in Christ' it is good also to realise that we have been looking at a very practical theme.

Often today it can seem that we live in a world falling apart. We are all aware of increased crime, violence and global terrorism. There is a continuing breakdown in respect for and honouring of authority. Many individuals' lives have been shaken by economic recession and unemployment in recent years. We have seen church leaders denying fundamental truths of the Christian faith and have viewed the British royal family beset with scandals and divorce.

God said that he would shake the earth (Hebrews 12:26), and certainly we can see everything in the earthly realm being shaken. But we belong to a different realm. 'In Christ' every blessing of the Holy Spirit is ours in the heavenly realm. The realm and kingdom to which we belong cannot be shaken to pieces – it will stand.

What is God doing?

What is God doing in the earth today? Jesus made the answer very clear when he declared that he would build his church.

There is a call in this book to take the promise of Jesus seriously. What Jesus has promised to do is what he will do until the very last day of history. I believe that to be part of the church is therefore to be part of the most important work that God is doing on the earth today. The church is the very epicentre of God's focus and attention. Nothing can be more worthwhile than to be a part of what God is giving such attention to upon the earth.

We can criticise the church and grow weary of what we see as its failures and shortcomings, but God himself is committed to it and Jesus is building it.

At the very end of history there will be the restoration of the whole of creation and even the reason for that is intimately connected with the church. In the Book of Revelation we see the church, described as the new Jerusalem, prepared as a bride beautifully dressed for her husband, descending from heaven to a new earth. (See Revelation 21:1–2.)

Surely, there can be nothing more important at the present time than seeing the church shape up more and more to her description in the scriptures. The world needs local churches with the qualities and the evident presence of God that will astonish towns and cities. We need to battle, as God gives us grace, for the restoration of the church.

Chapter 2   **Demonstration**
God's wisdom displayed to the world

At Stoneleigh Bible Week in 1995 I was attending a Leaders' Seminar that ended with a time of passionate prayer for church planting and church growth in London. I had grown up in North London, but I also had friends in St Albans just to the north of London. While we were praying I had an overwhelming impression that I should write to these friends, John and Valerie. I knew that they had attended Spring Harvest weeks and wanted to experience a more vibrant church life and I also suspected that they did not quite know what to do. However my reason for contacting John and Valerie was not the result of trying to analyse their situation, but because I really felt that God was telling me to do it.

I wrote them a rather general letter asking if they had any plans for the future and expressing the hope that we could help them in some way. They replied by saying that they had picked up my letter as they returned from renewal meetings in Toronto! Very soon they were meeting with some friends on a Friday evening and then, having slowly grown in numbers, moved a few years later to a Sunday morning meeting. About a year later I went to preach at a service where they were welcomed as a Newfrontiers church planting. At the end of 2002 I preached there again when the church appointed their first full-time elder.

This may not sound a very remarkable story, but because I feel such a passion for the local church, it was thrilling for me to have been involved in a time of prayer at Stoneleigh, then see a tiny church planted and grow to a point where they were able to support their first full-time worker.

The vision that is described in this book is not simply about seeing new churches planted, or even old churches vamped up a bit, but rather to see the church as a whole demonstrate and experience something more of the life that we read about in the New Testament.

For over three decades the local church has been my passion and love in ministry. I bear some scars, because passion and love make one vulnerable to being hurt. There have been the disappointments and the inevitable relationship breakdowns. Love hurts, but building church is real life. Alongside the pain there is joy, alongside the lows there are also the highs, and alongside the routine there is also the adventure.

What does it mean to be the church?

We demonstrate Christ to one another

In 1 Corinthians 12 we have Paul's well-known description of the church as the body of Christ. We often hear that this is Paul's favourite picture of the church, but it is more than a picture. If it was just a picture Paul would probably simply say: 'Now, you are a body', but not more than that. And at one level Paul is giving us a picture, and it is an easy one to visualise. A body is complete, but it is made up of many parts – toes, arms, a nose and so on. All the parts belong to the body and together they make the body a whole. Seen like this we understand that the apostle is teaching that we are interdependent members in the church, and so making it clear that all the members need one another.

We can however, make the picture a problem when we become over-concerned as to which part of the body we are. Am I an eye or a finger? Obviously the preacher is the mouth! But this concern is not Paul's emphasis. We should never be thinking that I am inferior and therefore frustrated because I want to be something else in the body. We are all parts of the body, and we need each other.

But neither can I take a superior attitude and become dismissive of others by taking the attitude that I do not need someone else who is in fact part of the body. In the church we are interdependent, and Paul gives us this picture of the body to help us see this.

But he is giving us more than a picture when he says, 'Now you are the body of Christ ...' (1 Corinthians 12:27). This tells us more than that we are interdependent and needing one another; we are actually something of Christ to one another. If we put our hand to our mouth then we are offering something of ourselves to our mouth. So, in the church, we can offer something of Christ to one another, and we do it in different ways because we are different parts of the body.

In the last section of 1 Corinthians 12 Paul asks whether all are apostles, or prophets or teachers, and the answer he expects, which is clear in the Greek text, is a definite, 'no'. But some are apostles, or prophets, or teachers, and what they bring to the church brings something of Christ to the church. If we bring gifts of administration or a word of knowledge, then we bring something of Christ to the rest of the body.

When a woman I know in our church, who has no high profile in public ministry, is seen to be cooking meals, looking after children, helping the sick in our congregation year in year out, then she is demonstrating something of Christ to the rest of the body.

In the church we do not just function or take part; that would make us *any body*. We are the *body of Christ* and so we demonstrate Christ to one another. So, if we need encouragement, Jesus does not send us a postcard, but someone in the body may bring a prophecy or a teaching that lifts our spirit and shows something of Christ to us. Of course it also means if we are negative or unkind to others within the church then we fail to show Christ to one another.

Jesus Christ, the Son of God, came in human flesh as a man who went about doing good. The church is the flesh and blood body of Christ now on the earth, and as parts of the body we show Christ to one another.

We often claim that the church is not a building, but neither is it the Sunday meeting. It is the body of Christ.

This is why the New Testament makes it clear that love is the lifeblood of the church, for love was the overwhelming mark of Christ's ministry. 1 Corinthians 13 emphasises that spiritual gifts are meaningless and empty without love. So, we are not just meant to function and participate, but as the body of Christ to function in love to one another and therefore to show Christ to one another.

We demonstrate Christ to the world

More extraordinary than being the body of Christ is what Paul says about the church in verse 12 of 1 Corinthians 12: 'The body is a unit, though it is made up of many parts; and though all its parts are many, they form one body. So it is with Christ.' There is a surprise in that last phrase. We would expect to read: 'So it is with the body of Christ.' Paul in fact calls the church, 'Christ'. Sometimes commentators suggest that 'Christ' here means the church as a shortened form of 'body of Christ'. In other words Paul is just using an abbreviation here.

But I would suggest it is more deliberate than that. In Acts 9, Saul (later Paul) encounters Christ on the Damascus Road and Jesus asks why he is persecuting *him*, when actually Paul was persecuting the church. And in verse 5 the Lord continues, 'I am Jesus, whom you are persecuting.' So to persecute the church is to persecute Jesus. That is how closely the Lord identifies himself with the church. When in 1 Corinthians 12 Paul calls the church: 'Christ', then it carries the idea that the church is Christ on the earth. This may be hard for us to grasp fully, but it is certainly more than a nice spiritual thought; rather it means that the church should be showing Christ to the world.

When Jesus came in the flesh, he came in a body that walked and talked. People could see Jesus; they could listen to him, and could watch him. What chance does the world have to see Jesus now? Every chance! The church is Christ on the earth, and the church is the way the world is able to see Jesus.

Through personal witness an individual Christian can make an impression on someone else by his or her quality and integrity of life. But it is often when a non-believer meets with a community of Christians that he or she can be far more impressed. This is not to suggest that the meeting has to be a Sunday morning meeting, but simply being involved with Christians at a social level can make an impact. There is something to be demonstrated through the quality of our life together. In my own church, during the summer, we have picnics together in our local parks and have often found these are a very good way of introducing non-believers to our faith, by first letting them experience a community of Christians relating together.

We have also run four-day summer festivals in our city providing free entertainment, bouncy castles and sports opportunities for thousands of people. We now have members of our church who first met us as a community of believers, but not in a Sunday meeting.

This does not mean that everyone will like what he or she sees as the church. Not everyone liked Jesus when they met him. He had strong and persistent enemies who were eventually to have the death penalty imposed on him. The church has her enemies and faces hostility and there are those who would like to impose the death penalty on the church and get her out of the way. But we are Christ to the world and we bring society the truth.

This is a generation that is being lied to. I once read in a Sunday newspaper that virginity is a gift to be given away at 16: that is a lie. We are told that the best way to deal with an inconvenient pregnancy is through an abortion: that is a lie. There are those who claim that gay sex is normal: that is a lie. To believe that money equals happiness is to be taken in by a lie.

To write like this is not a matter of being traditional, or conservative with old-fashioned and outdated religious attitudes. We are talking of a pack of lies that is being forced upon our generation. In contrast to this there is the truth that the church, representing Christ on the earth, is to live out and to bring to our generation. The truth sets people free, while lies mess us up.

At the same time we have to remember that Christ was never against people but he could be against the things that they did. Jesus told the woman taken in adultery to sin no more, but he was not against her. So the church always accepts people, whatever they have done. Look at the kind of people who made up the church in Corinth:

> ... Do not be deceived: Neither the sexually immoral nor idolaters nor adulterers nor male prostitutes nor homosexual offenders nor thieves nor the greedy nor drunkards nor slanderers nor swindlers will inherit the kingdom of God. And that is what some of you were ... (1 Corinthians 6:9–11).

The church at Corinth had accepted people who had done all those things and the church accepts them still today.

We must not fall for the suggestion that we proclaim truth simply as we see it. That is exactly what it is not. It is the truth as God sees it. We are not proclaiming ever-changing truth; we are talking of God's eternal truth. So we are not soft in our pre-sentation of truth, but we are Christ to the world.

The truth never made Christ harsh and so the church is never to be like that. Through the family of churches I belong to, we are bringing the compassion and love of Christ to many countries through social action, housing schemes, through feeding the hungry and training the poor in various skills to enable them to get work. In the city of Mumbai with its 160,000 leprosy sufferers we have vans going around the city equipped to offer these people showers, medical treatment, and physical human contact. This is typical of what the body of Christ is doing across the world.

The church demonstrates Christ to the world.

We demonstrate Christ to the universe

This is a claim that definitely sounds rather far-fetched. We speak of demonstrating Christ to one another and to the world through the church and now we are off into the cosmos somewhere!

But if this sounds like an exaggeration it is one that Paul, himself, was certainly prone to: 'His intent was that now, through the church, the manifold wisdom of God should be made known to the rulers and authorities in the heavenly realms' (Ephesians 3:10).

Who are these rulers and authorities? Well, most commentators would argue on the basis of other scriptures that they are angels and demons. So, God's purpose is that right now the church should be demonstrating God's manifold wisdom, which is essentially Christ and the transforming work that he does to angels and demons; yes, to cosmic powers.

How can this be done? We have already seen that the church is the body of Christ and so we demonstrate God's manifold wisdom by being his body. The church shows the revolutionary work of Christ in many lives that are not only reconciled to God, but also to one another. It is simply the church truly being church, and that is really a repeated theme in this book.

The church is a community of radically changed people. These people have been reconciled to God, and despite differences in education, career, skin colour and a variety of other issues that often divide people, they have been brought together by Christ. It is now a community of faith to do big exploits and to enjoy worshipping an invisible God. How does this happen? Jesus has worked the transformation in countless individuals through his sacrifice and redeeming work on the cross. Angels must view such a community with huge pleasure for there they see the wisdom of God and what he has done. Demons must hate it.

So the church demonstrates Christ to the universe in the sense of showing the wisdom of God to cosmic powers.

We will be the bride of Christ

The church may be the body of Christ now, but one day she will become the bride. If we try to be too analytical at this point we could hit a problem. How can that which is presently the body of Christ and can even be called Christ change to become the bride of Christ?

We need to recognise that the church is so magnificently the work of God that she transcends human logic and analysis. The best way that the New Testament can describe the future destiny of the church in a fashion that we can understand is to say that the church marries Christ. The celebrations of that occasion are described in Revelation 19:6,7:

> *Then I heard what sounded like a great multitude, like the roar of rushing waters and like loud peals of thunder, shouting: 'Hallelujah! For our Lord God Almighty reigns. Let us rejoice and be glad and give him glory! For the wedding of the Lamb has come, and his bride has made herself ready.'*

However there is another fascinating element to all this described in chapter 21, verse 9. 'One of the seven angels who had the seven bowls full of the seven last plagues came and said to me. "Come, I will show you the bride, the wife of the Lamb."' Here the angel actually calls John's attention to the church.

It is very easy in our so-called post-Christian society for a local church to feel small, irrelevant, beleaguered and unable to make much progress. We can bemoan the fact that we are, say, just 50 people in a town of 100,000 people. It can cause us to have a low self-image. But this mighty angel in the book of Revelation calls our attention to the magnificent bride, the work of God, the redeemed community of the King.

During his ministry John the Baptist pointed to Christ and said: 'Behold the Lamb of God'. In heaven that Lamb will stand in the centre of the throne to occupy our gaze forever. We will be totally captivated and will cry out: 'Worthy is the Lamb that was slain.' So we will look at him, the Lamb of God.

But the angel says to John, 'Look at the bride, the wife of the Lamb.' Only a people washed clean by the blood of the Lamb can appear spotless and beautiful in heaven. This is the church, the bride who is to be joined to Christ for eternal celebrations.

One day the whole universe is going to be rearranged for this bride. 'And God placed all things under his feet and appointed him to be head over everything for the church, which is his body, the fulness of him who fills everything in every way' (Ephesians 1:22,23). Christ is head over everything for his body, his bride, that is the church. So one day there will be a new heaven and earth to accommodate the bride.

We can turn up to a church meeting on a Sunday without much faith or expectation, or we can come half-heartedly to a midweek prayer meeting. We can even feel weary and disappointed with the church. But the Bible tells us we are the body of Christ and everyone who is a believer is part of it. There is a glory and dignity and majesty about the church that needs to capture our attention and therefore our wholehearted involvement.

We are a demonstration of Christ to one another, to the world, and to cosmic powers. And we will be with Christ forever.

When Jesus said he would build his church, he was speaking rock solid truth. He is doing it around the world right now and he will do it until the day he comes again. Christ's passion for the church ought therefore to be our passion.

We can be passionate for many other things in life. We may be enthusiastically committed to our career or to a sport or to travel. However, it is unlikely we will ever achieve all that we want to in these areas. Those passions should be exceeded by a greater passion for the most important thing that God is doing on this earth. We are talking about the church.

Chapter 3   # Salvation
Saved to belong

The church is not a club. It's not an association of like-minded people. It comprises only those people who know Jesus Christ as Saviour and Lord. In speaking of the church, we must therefore talk about salvation. Unless Christ genuinely saves people, there is no church.

Referring to Paul's teaching on salvation in Romans 3:21–26 Martin Luther commented that it is 'the chief point ... of the whole Bible'. Dr Martyn Lloyd-Jones commented on it as 'the heart of the Epistle' (to the Romans). John Piper says, 'verses 25,26 are, perhaps, the most central and most important part of the Bible'. It can hardly be overstated, therefore, that this is a key passage. It is worth breaking down this passage into small sections.

Righteousness from God

> *But now a righteousness from God, apart from law, has been made known, to which the Law and the Prophets testify (v. 21).*

Paul begins Romans with some introductory remarks and then right through from chapter 1:18, and up to this verse, the Apostle has been spelling out the truth that no one is righteous in the sight of God. In fact, verse 23 produces a summary of his teaching: 'For all have sinned and fall short of the glory of God'.

That is the position of all men and women, and Paul has previously been at pains to emphasise it. Man's sin is demonstrated in his failure to keep the Law, an argument that early Jewish readers would have been able to connect with. The Jews had the law; they knew the Ten Commandments that God had delivered to Moses. But no Jew, and no other man or woman has succeeded in perfectly keeping the Law of God.

However, the Law is not just to be understood in a formal sense as the Law of Moses. It represents a whole system of man's own efforts.

Basically what it comes to is this: whether we have the Ten Commandments or seek to follow a particular moral code, or even our own philosophy of how to live, the onus is always on us to succeed. I am the one that needs to live it out, and I fail to do so. This is the reason that God is unable to view any person as righteous.

So, life's biggest question, whether men and women know it or not, is always, 'How can I get right with God?' This verse provides the answer in one simple statement when it says: 'But now a righteousness from God, apart from the law, has been made known.'

Here we have a total shift in both human history and understanding. People's views on salvation, or on how a person becomes acceptable to God, have always been for self-based efforts. It is always a matter of what they have done, or what they can do.

But this is an entirely different perspective and it is what makes Christianity unique. In fact, righteousness comes to us from God; it does not proceed from us towards God.

So when Paul begins verse 21 with 'But now' this is a thundering attention grabber. In the past, the Jews attempted to reach God through doing the works of the law. In history, men and women have always had a 'do-it-yourself' approach to salvation. Right now the comment we often hear is something like, 'Well, I think if there is a God I will have done enough for the scales to come down in my favour'. But now, it is altogether different as we see that righteousness comes to us from God apart from any works of the law or our own efforts.

Every believer is a fruit of this 'But now'. There has been a fundamental change. It is no longer, what can I do to get right with God? Rather, God's righteousness is given to me.

In the past (v. 21 speaks of the time of the Law and the Prophets) there was a witness to this new era that would come. The Old Testament scriptures do speak of this way of God's dealing with people. Chapter 4 of Romans gives us examples. 'What does the Scripture say? "Abraham believed God, and it was credited to him as righteousness"' (v. 3). So, Abraham did not achieve a righteous standing before God on the basis of his works.

Again, 'David says the same thing when he speaks of the blessedness of the man to whom God credits righteousness apart from works' (v. 6). So, even in the Old Testament we get a glimpse of what is to become fully disclosed in the New Testament about this matter. Now we are given the full revelation – righteousness comes to us from God.

Through faith

This righteousness from God comes through faith in Jesus Christ to all who believe. There is no difference (Romans 3:22).

Faith is the means by which the righteousness from God is applied to us.

We must be careful not to see our faith as a work, for it is really an abandonment of dependence on self and a trust in what only God can do. Faith is not a matter of me making an effort, it is a surrender. Faith means I acknowledge that I am incapable of getting right with God through my own works, I depend entirely on God. So God-given righteousness is applied to our lives through faith.

This is universally true, for Paul says of faith, 'There is no difference'. We may come from Africa or America, we may be very rich or very poor, we may be Jew or Gentile, but there is no difference when it comes to faith. For all who give up on themselves and trust in Christ alone, this is the way and indeed the only way of salvation.

Why are so many people offended by the Christian message? Christians speak of one way to God. To some this can sound intolerant and arrogant. But we are not talking of anything we do, for that could certainly open us up to the charge of arrogance. We have given up on ourselves to put our trust in Christ alone.

All have sinned

for all have sinned and fall short of the glory of God (v. 23).

So whereas God's righteousness is applied to all who believe and there is no difference, there is no difference either in that all have sinned and fall short of the glory of God.

Again, we may be American or African, rich or poor, Jew or Gentile, but we are all sinners before God. To fall short of God's glory probably means to move away from the image of God in which we were all made. All of us have done that.

So we have a reminder here that we all need God's righteousness, for all of us have sinned and fallen short of God's glory. This is our real problem and it is the reason we need God. It is no good proclaiming a message of 'come to Jesus' unless we are clear at this point. To say: 'Come to Jesus and all your problems disappear' is nonsense. To say: 'Come to Jesus and everything will then be joy and wonder' does not take account of the illness or even tragedy that so many Christians face.

It is not even very attractive to invite people to Jesus so that they can be part of the church. Just think of all those meetings! We really have to start with the recognition that we have sinned and fallen short. We have broken the law of God and messed up even by our own standards. We were in desperate trouble because there is just punishment and condemnation for lawlessness. Our position was utterly hopeless until God intervened and then we received righteousness from him.

That changes everything. Now we can rejoice even in times of huge loss. I've seen and know believers who've tragically lost a child and are living constantly with the searing pain of that and yet still rejoicing in the wonder of their salvation.

Now it makes sense to be part of the church, for we share a common salvation experience with the other members of the community.

However we have sinned and fallen short. We were not just inconvenienced, we were condemned. 'But now', a righteousness from God is revealed; the complete answer that we needed.

Four words

> *and are justified freely by his grace through the redemption that came by Christ Jesus (v. 24).*

This verse explains exactly how God's righteousness is able to come to us. The individual words here are of real importance.

Justified

This word comes from the same root as the word 'righteous'. So, to be justified is to be declared righteous.

Therefore, when we talk of righteousness coming from God it means that we are justified. To say we are justified makes it clear that we cannot justify ourselves. We are acknowledging what God has done. And very importantly this is not saying we are made righteous, but that we are declared righteous.

If we interpret justification as being made righteous by God, then we have an immediate problem. We could object on the grounds that we still get angry or that we still feel impatient or we could rehearse a thousand other deficiencies we are aware of in ourselves. But justification declares us righteous before any moral change has taken place in our life. The moment we believe in Christ there is an acquittal and release from all the charges stacked up against us because of our sin. There is a judicial or legal verdict that declares that we are set free from all condemnation. We are declared to be righteous. Sanctification is the lifelong process to make us righteous that follows justification.

Freely
If justification sounds rather scandalous because we are declared righteous without any moral change, it can now be seen as a greater scandal still! We cannot do anything to pay for being declared righteous. For justification is a gift, it comes to us for free.

Grace
Justification is seen as even more amazing as Paul now introduces the word 'grace'. We can understand grace by a statement made in the next chapter. 'Now when a man works, his wages are not credited to him as a gift, but as an obligation' (4:4).

If you work for someone, you do not get grace; you get wages. They are owed to you. Grace is the good we get from someone who owes us nothing. God owes us nothing, but he gives us grace, his undeserved and unmerited favour. So we cannot pay for righteousness and we cannot work for righteousness, it is grace.

Redemption
The doctrine of justification can appear very unfair. What justice is there in declaring people to be righteous who have fallen so short of God's glory and in whom there has been no moral change?

The answer is provided here in the word 'redemption'. In

biblical times it was possible to redeem someone from slavery by the payment of a ransom. This ransom was a sum of money that bought someone out of slavery and delivered him into freedom.

We are familiar with this idea today. A person is captured by a group of terrorists. The payment of a ransom is demanded to purchase his freedom. Often today, the price demanded will be the release from prison of some friends of the terrorists.

We were once held in slavery, both to sin and to the condemnation that follows sin. Now, a ransom has been paid and so we are redeemed from slavery and set free. That ransom price is the blood of Jesus and he paid it when he gave up his life on the cross.

For us still to be held in slavery when the ransom has been fully paid is what would be totally unjust. For our freedom we owe everything to the death of Jesus Christ.

If we were kidnapped by terrorists and held in a dark room, wondering every moment if we were going to be tortured or put to death, then our situation would be desperate and we would be living in constant fear. Imagine that one day we were told that someone had paid a ransom for us and we were free to go; we would be overjoyed.

Jesus has paid up – he has paid in full. We are free.

Atonement

> *God presented him as a sacrifice of atonement, through faith in his blood. He did this to demonstrate his justice, because in his forbearance he had left the sins committed beforehand unpunished – he did it to demonstrate his justice at the present time, so as to be just and the one who justifies those who have faith in Jesus (vv. 25,26).*

Every year, on the Day of Atonement, the High Priest of Israel would enter the Holy of Holies. On this most holy day in all

Jewish religion, he would sprinkle the blood of animal sacrifice upon the altar. This blood from a life that had been given in sacrifice would turn aside the wrath of God against the sins of the nation of Israel.

When Paul says that Christ is the sacrifice of atonement he is saying that Christ is both the person and the place of sacrifice. We see the mention of blood, but now we are not talking of the blood of animal sacrifice, but rather the sacrifice of the eternal Son of God. The blood of this sacrifice turns aside the wrath of God against our sins and Jesus took that wrath on himself as he died on the cross at Calvary. Because he is the eternal Son, he turns aside God's wrath from us forever.

Once again, we see God's initiative in all of this, for it was God who presented Jesus as a sacrifice. Christ did not unfortunately die and then the disciples had to find an explanation for such a terrible event. It was God's intention to bruise his Son. He was given to be the sacrifice that would turn God's wrath from our sin.

'The prime doer in Christ's cross was God. Christ was God reconciling. He was God doing the very best for man and not man doing his very best for God' (P.E. Hughes).[1]

A big question

We are still left with a question. Why does God, overall, seem to have treated sin so lightly? We read the account of Nathan's exposure of King David's sin in his adultery with Bathsheba and the subsequent murder of Uriah. What we see is David getting off relatively easily. Nathan says to David, 'The Lord has taken away your sin. You are not going to die' (2 Samuel 12:13).

So, is God really quite light on sin? We can think of really evil men who seem to get away with doing terrible things. Doesn't God care about his name and his glory? The reality is, God is never soft on sin. He punishes it ruthlessly and completely.

As believers, our sin was ruthlessly and completely

punished in the death of the Son of God. But every sin is punished in full and if it is not punished in Christ, it will be punished in eternity. So, God is just; for all sin is punished. But God, himself, has provided this great salvation. He justifies, or he declares righteous, all those who have faith in Jesus.

A great salvation

In this passage we have an explanation for why men are as they are and why the world is as it is. All have sinned and fallen short of God's glory. But we also have the very essence of the gospel explained. A righteousness from God has been made known. It is applied to us through faith. It became possible because the blood of Christ is the ransom price paid to set us free. It is effective because Christ has turned aside the wrath of God and has taken God's full anger against our sin upon himself.

We also have great security. This great salvation is the result of God's initiative towards us. Righteousness comes from God. He justifies us, he declares us righteous. God has provided Jesus as a sacrifice of atonement, so his wrath is turned away from our sins.

In a way, our faith stands in protest against all that opposes us. In the face of difficult circumstances, hostile people or the uncertainty of the world situation, we can proclaim God has declared us righteous.

Finally, we have a great sense of destiny. We know we have sinned and fallen short of God's glory. However, our great end time hope is that we shall be fully restored to all that we are meant to be in the image of God. We are not here just to grab what we can from this life, whether it is money or success or a better career. We are travellers in this life who are on our way to glory and to enjoying God through endless ages.

The message

There is no church community unless it comprises those who have been justified. Whatever we believe about the way the church should be demonstrating and experiencing the life of God, however passionate we may feel about the church, nothing is possible without individuals knowing this great salvation.

This message cannot be compromised or minimised. It is the essential element of the church being the church. We must do all we can to strengthen our understanding of the truth of salvation and to proclaim it as fully and as attractively as we can.

When God saves individuals he saves them into a community, which is the church. Believers are not called to live in isolation from other Christians, but are joined to the family of God. This family has its local expressions all over the world. As God's very own community the church should always have a passion to demonstrate the absolute wonder of salvation.

Note

1. *Paul's Second Epistle to the Corinthians*, P.E. Hughes, The New London Commentary on the New Testament. Marshall, Morgan and Scott, 1961.

Chapter 4   # Apostles
                 Given by Christ

Ask those who were around during the early years of the so-called Restoration movement or New Churches to open their Bibles, and they automatically fall open at Ephesians 4!

Certainly in the early Bible weeks such as the Dales and at the Downs, a great deal of teaching was given from this chapter. In the general belief that God was restoring certain truths to his church there was a conviction that this was true also of the ministries mentioned in Ephesians 4.

In Ephesians 4:11 we read of apostles, prophets, evangelists, and pastors and teachers. Pastors and teachers have always been recognised in the ministry of the local church. Evangelists have usually been considered as very helpful to the church from time to time, although years ago it was difficult to think of an evangelist without placing him in the Billy Graham mould.

But it was generally considered among evangelical churches that apostles and prophets belonged only to the New Testament era and indeed prophets were more Old Testament than New Testament. The argument that there are apostles and prophets ministering today has proved something of a battle for the New Churches, but one that they are probably winning by good biblical interpretation.

Ephesians 4

The key verse in this chapter for teaching that there are apostles today is clearly verse 11:

> *It was he who gave some to be apostles, some to be prophets,*
> *some to be evangelists, and some to be pastors and teachers.*

The critical point is identifying the 'he', which is the third word of the verse. At first sight there does not appear to be any issue here for the 'he' is surely 'Christ'. Any natural reading of the text makes that clear, for running on from verse 7 we are simply told what Christ has given to the church and this includes apostles. Absolutely nobody, including those who deny the existence of apostles today, offers any other suggestion than that the 'he' is Christ.

However, a careful study of these verses reveals that the 'he' is not just 'Christ', rather we are reading of the 'ascended Christ'. Paul says, 'When he ascended on high, he ... gave gifts to men' (v. 8). Again, 'He who descended is the very one who ascended ...' (v. 10). So verse 11 must be understood within its context as telling us that the ascended Christ gave some to be apostles. This is crucial, for if the *ascended* Christ gives apostles to the church, then there were apostles given to the church even in the New Testament era who did not belong to the original Twelve.

Indeed, because Christ has been ascended throughout church history we can also reason that Christ has been continually giving apostles to the church.

Apostles

The New Testament suggests that there are different types of apostles.

Firstly, Christ is *the* apostle. 'Therefore, holy brothers, who share in the heavenly calling, fix your thoughts on Jesus, the apostle and high priest whom we confess' (Hebrews 3:1). In the Greek language, 'apostle' means one who is sent. Supremely, Christ is the 'sent one' who has come into this world for our salvation. Obviously, Christ holds a unique position as the apostle of our faith.

Secondly, there are the Twelve Apostles. These were the twelve men chosen by Jesus to accompany him in his ministry and to receive instruction directly from him. What came to distinguish these twelve apostles was the fact that they were able to give a first-hand witness to the resurrection. This is clear from the way in which a selection process for a new apostle was held to replace Judas Iscariot. 'Therefore it is necessary to choose one of the men who have been with us the whole time the Lord Jesus went in and out among us, beginning from John's baptism to the time when Jesus was taken up from us. For one of these must become a witness with us of his resurrection' (Acts 1:21,22). Matthias was chosen as one of those who fitted this description.

The apostle Paul seems to be in a category of his own. He was not chosen to be an apostle while Jesus was on the earth, but he did see the risen Christ, and so was able, like the Twelve, to be a witness to the resurrection. Paul spoke of the appearance of the risen Christ to him on the Damascus Road (e.g. 1 Corinthians 15:8). However, Paul was not appointed as an apostle until Christ ascended to heaven. So Paul stands uniquely as an apostle who had seen the risen Christ but was also appointed by the ascended Christ.

Then we have the apostles of the ascension. These are men who did not witness the resurrection but whom the ascended Christ has given to the church to fulfil that ministry. Barnabas, Silas and Timothy (1 Thessalonians 2:6, Acts 14:14) are all called apostles in the New Testament even though they had not seen Christ raised from the dead. So there is no logical reason to doubt that the ascended Christ has continued, throughout history, to give apostles to the church.

It is certainly not being suggested here that Christ only started to give apostles to the church again in the mid-1960s with the rise of the new charismatic movement. John Wesley, William Carey, William Booth and numerous others can be seen in history as serving the church with this ministry. They established and cared for numbers of churches.

What does an apostle do?

An apostle is particularly gifted to help churches get well planted and well established. Paul refers to his ministry in terms of being an expert builder (1 Corinthians 3:10). He planted the churches at Corinth and Ephesus, but the account of his ministry in Acts and also his letters to these churches make it clear that his desire was to see them well established.

A specific example of an ongoing concern for the churches that have been planted can be seen in his comment to Titus: 'The reason I left you in Crete was that you might straighten out what was left unfinished and appoint elders in every town, as I directed you' (Titus 1:5).

So Paul saw the need to straighten things out. Local churches can sometimes drift off course, not necessarily by teaching wrong doctrine, but in failing to bring the whole counsel of God. Paul had to write to the church at Corinth and straighten them out in the area of speaking in tongues. We can see that in 1 Corinthians 14. An apostle can discern where matters need to be brought into order.

Paul speaks to Titus of that which is 'unfinished'. There is always unfinished work in a church. A church may be neglecting or failing to reach some aspect of its vision. An apostle can see this and encourage the church and its leaders to give some attention here or there. A church will have a commitment to pray, but the apostle may discern that the church has become weak or discouraged in this area. He can point out the need and help bring the church through in this part of its vision.

Paul also had a concern for the appointing of leaders. It is not the greatest wisdom for existing elders to appoint more elders without another's help or counsel. The leaders will need the apostle's wisdom, experience and also his ability to ask the right questions concerning any man who is being considered for eldership.

Apostolic authority

The use of apostolic authority can be a sensitive and misunderstood issue.

It is very clear from the New Testament that elders lead a local church. We should expect that God will raise up a team of elders who oversee each church community. The idea that a particular church belongs to an apostle is foreign to the New Testament. It is true that an apostle may be an elder of a particular church – the apostle Peter referred to himself as an elder (1 Peter 5:1), and Paul was clearly the senior leader of the church during his three-year stay in Ephesus. But an apostle has a gifting that is always causing him to look to the far horizon and he wants to break through into a new area.

It is not usually a good idea therefore for an apostle to be the long-term senior leader of a church; his gifting will mean that in time he will begin to neglect the church he is leading because he is looking to see another church planted. But as the apostle moves among the churches, those who relate to him will have leaders that recognise his apostolic authority.

We have already seen that Paul instructed Titus to straighten out what was left unfinished in the churches in Crete and to appoint elders. He also writes to Titus: 'You must teach what is in accord with sound doctrine. Teach the older men to be temperate, worthy of respect, self-controlled and sound in faith, in love and in endurance' (Titus 2:1,2). In 1 Corinthians Paul gives instructions to a church that is being very lax in dealing with serious sin by one of the members. We can imagine the leaders really snapping to attention when Paul writes: 'When you are assembled in the name of our Lord Jesus and I am with you in spirit, and the power of our Lord Jesus is present, hand this man over to Satan, so that the sinful nature may be destroyed and his spirit saved on the day of the Lord' (1 Corinthians 5:4,5).

So Paul did not hold back in his exercise of authority through the giving of instructions. However, the purpose of such authority is made clear when Paul writes: 'This is why I write these things when I am absent, that when I come I may not have to be harsh in my use of authority – the authority the Lord gave me for building you up, not for tearing you down' (2 Corinthians 13:10). If we want our church built up, it is healthy to submit to apostolic authority.

It is a spiritual authority

Paul says, 'I may not be a trained speaker, but I do have knowledge ...' (2 Corinthians 11:6). Some men go through a great deal of training for ministry. They go to college, take a degree, and maybe pursue further theological research. They can be highly educated but prove to be totally inept when it comes to leading a church.

I know other men who have not passed a single exam in their lives, who have no theological degrees or formal training of any kind, yet they have a God given wisdom about building local churches. A friend of mine with no academic or formal theological qualifications has planted two of the biggest churches in Newfrontiers in Hastings and Eastbourne in the past 25 years. There is a spiritual authority that is essential for the apostle, something given by God that is not conferred by a theological degree.

I am not opposed to theological study, indeed I organise and teach on many training courses myself, but I am aware that it does not result in automatic spiritual authority.

It is a biblical authority

Apostolic authority must always line up with the scriptures. So, to stand down an elder who is guilty of serious sin and remains unrepentant is biblical. The Bible teaches us about discipline in the church. But to demand, say, that every church leader must conduct all his correspondence by e-mail would not be biblical. The latter may be sensible, but spiritual authority cannot be exercised in areas where the Bible does not give us instruction or direction.

It is a real authority

Sometimes an apostle will simply talk things through with a team of elders. Relationships are very important and an apostle and a group of elders will genuinely seek to be friends together. Paul's farewell to the elders at Ephesus (Acts 20) reveals just how deep the levels of friendship and affection were among them. But there are times when an apostle will give direction and the authority needs to be recognised and responded to.

It is important to understand that an apostle will lay down principles, but it will be for the local elders to work out the details. So, an apostle could say that he believes it is necessary for the elders to give much more attention to the prayer life of the church. Elders who are wise will submit to his counsel. However, it could be very unhelpful for the apostle, say, to prescribe a three-hour prayer meeting every Friday evening. The elders who will know the church community well – for they are the leaders – may be aware of various reasons why this would simply be a bad idea. It is their responsibility to work out the details.

It can be delegated authority

Again, we recall Paul's words to Titus to straighten out what was unfinished and for him to appoint elders. Titus was charged by the apostle to carry out an apostolic work. We can also see this delegated authority when Paul writes: 'So when we could stand it no longer, we thought it best to be left by ourselves in Athens. We sent Timothy who is our brother and God's fellow worker in spreading the gospel of Christ, to strengthen and encourage you in your faith' (1 Thessalonians 3:1,2).

Later in the same chapter Paul tells how Timothy reports back to him after a successful visit. How does delegated authority work? Well, these churches obviously trusted the apostle Paul. If the apostle they trusted sent to them a man whom he trusted, then they would be able to trust that man as well. The reality is that a particular apostle may have so many ministry demands upon his life that he has to involve other trustworthy men to assist him.

If the ascended Christ had not given to the church men of apostolic authority throughout her history, then it is hard to imagine how she would have broken through into many new areas.

Pastors naturally seek to protect and guard and maintain the church that God has called them to. In the next chapter we will comment on the value of this. Pastors are not often great risk takers who want to move out and seize new ground. The apostolic ministry again and again is the key to new breakthrough.

It was an apostle who said, 'So from Jerusalem all the way round to Illyricum, I have fully proclaimed the gospel of Christ. It has always been my ambition to preach the gospel where Christ was not known' (Romans 15:19,20). Then again, Paul writes these extraordinary words: 'But now that there is no more place for me to work in these regions, and since I have been longing for many years to see you, I plan to do so when I go to Spain ...' (Romans 15:23,24). Paul was constantly on the move, looking for new areas where he could preach the gospel and plant churches.

Like Paul?

Some people fear that believing in apostles today could mean a claim that a particular brother is like the apostle Paul or that he has the authority to write infallible Scripture today. We are not going to claim that anyone today is remotely of the stature of Paul until he has been imprisoned several times, flogged several times, shipwrecked, stoned, and has performed a number of outstanding miracles in the name of Jesus. Even then we would be looking for many churches to have been planted and well established.

But even so, no apostle today could claim to have seen the

risen Christ. To state that someone today has an apostolic ministry and that therefore he is another Paul would be fairly ridiculous.

As for the writing of Scripture; well, the canon closed itself about 1800 years ago and the early church fathers were then able to discern what was truly God-breathed. All the revelation we need for salvation and life is already in the Bible; we do not need anything to be written in addition.

However, if new churches are going to be planted, if we are going to reach every people group, as Jesus said, if churches are going to be well established, and if wise and godly leaders are to be raised up, then we need the apostolic ministry. It is the ascended Christ who gives such a gift; we do well to recognise it gladly and receive the ministry of the apostle that Christ sends to the church.

Chapter 5   # Ministries
Sent to serve

Christians can easily be accused of having their own 'in-house' jargon. Preachers are often requested to break away from religious language so that they can communicate more effectively with today's generation.

There is some potential danger here. Such requests for non-religious, jargon-free preaching can make those who publicly teach the word of God nervous of using some key theological terms like 'justification'. The reality is that the present generation has not been slow to adopt a whole new vocabulary that goes with the computer age. Such expressions as 'software', 'motherboard' and 'service provider' are phrases that most of us were totally unaware of a few years back. We need to take care not to expunge some vital biblical terms from our vocabulary in the name of becoming relevant; when in fact, to do so, could rob the gospel of its content.

At the same time I am aware that each denomination or family of churches is almost certain to develop something of its own vocabulary. This becomes very evident if you visit a church or a conference hosted by a stream different from your own. And sometimes various streams of churches use the same terms differently. For example, both Baptists and Anglicans use the term 'baptism', but there is a very great difference in what the word is understood to mean in its application. Again, with the word 'elder', we find that elders in the United Reformed Church are not viewed in the same way as elders in a Brethren Assembly.

Among the New Churches, we have coined the term

'Ephesians 4 Ministries' and that certainly needs some explanation.

Ephesians 4

I may appear to be breaking rank somewhat here, but I need to
state that there is no such thing as 'Ephesians 4 Ministries'. It
has become part of the jargon of particular groups of churches
and it is a phrase that in some ways is not very helpful.

It would be much more accurate to speak of the ministries
that we read of in Ephesians 4, but I suspect that is not snappy
enough to catch on. I am certainly not trying to be pedantic
here; it is an area where we need real clarity. When Paul wrote
to the church at Ephesus the phrase 'Ephesians 4 Ministries'
would never have crossed his mind, for the simple reason that
he did not write Ephesians 4, he was writing one unbroken letter undivided by chapters and verses.

When in the course of church history, and with the worthy
motivation of giving ease of reference to any part of the Bible,
chapters and verses were added in, then Ephesians 4 became
the place in the Bible where we read of Christ's gifts to the
church of apostles, prophets, evangelists, and pastors and
teachers. We are not being told that Christ gave 'Ephesians 4
Ministries' to the church, but he gave ministries to the church.

This is important because the term 'Ephesians 4 Ministries'
can become elitist and also lead to the mistaken view that
all these ministries are itinerant. The situation is most obvious
in referring to the so-called 'Ephesians 4 pastor/teacher'
although it does apply to some extent to both evangelists and
prophets.

If we speak of an Ephesians 4 pastor/teacher, we can give
the impression that there are other pastor/teachers who are
not of the stature of Ephesians 4 pastor/teachers. I am inclined,
tongue in cheek, to refer to them as Ephesians 2 pastor/teachers.
But the Ephesians 4 pastor/teacher is regarded as being of
another order and rank above the other pastor/teachers.

Usually this then gets extended with a conviction that what particularly marks out the Ephesians 4 pastor/teacher is that he has an itinerant role, whereas those who are seen as having less than an Ephesians 4 standing have a settled role within the local church.

This cannot be what the text is saying. Ignoring the Ephesians 4 designation, we are simply reading that the ascended Christ has given different ministries to help the church and these ministries include prophets, evangelists, and pastor/teachers. It is true that a mixture of gifting, anointing, and experience may result in greater demand for a particular ministry, so that say, a very gifted pastor/teacher may travel to other churches very often, but this does not mean he is Ephesians 4 while other pastor/teachers are not. All pastor/teachers are a gift to the church from the ascended Christ.

In the last chapter we looked particularly at the role of the apostle; we need to give some attention here to the other ministries.

Prophets

We do not have a large amount of material in the New Testament on this subject, but there is enough to make it clear that prophets are not just confined to the Old Testament era.

Agabus is probably the best known prophet of the New Testament. We read in Acts 21 that he warned Paul of his impending arrest in Jerusalem. Earlier, this same prophet had foretold a famine that occurred during the reign of the Emperor Claudius and at that point he is mentioned as being one of a group of prophets (Acts 11:27).

Also in Acts 21 we read of Philip's four daughters who prophesied. Apart from making evenings at home very interesting before the advent of television, the specific reference must mean that they did rather more than bring the occasional devotional thought. Their prophesying is likely to have been at the level of something so substantial in content and anointing that they would have been recognised to be prophets.

This touches on an issue that is not easy to resolve fully. Bearing in mind that prophecy is a spiritual gift and that any member of the body of Christ might bring a prophecy, what is it that distinguishes a person's prophesying in a way that allows us to call them a prophet? Although intangible to some extent, it must have to do with content and anointing.

A prophet tends to arrest our attention in a way beyond those who from time to time prophesy in a meeting. Some years ago a prophet in our church brought a word during a prayer meeting about our need to prepare for God bringing a period of disruption to us. As elders we simply knew that God had spoken to us and we called the church to a season of prayer as a result. Within weeks God moved powerfully among us, disrupting (and lengthening) our meetings for a period of several months during which many of our congregation encountered God in a fresh and powerful way.

In Ephesians 2:20, Paul speaks of the church being 'built on the foundation of the apostles and prophets, with Christ Jesus himself as the chief cornerstone'. Now although some want to argue that the prophets here are to be understood as the writings of the Old Testament prophets, the fact that there were prophets in the New Testament period makes it perfectly valid to see these prophets being referred to here.

Indeed if we recognise that the ascended Christ is giving ministries of apostles and prophets to the church throughout her history, then it is logical to state that living apostles and prophets lay down the foundations for the local church today. Some suggest that this is only what the verse means, but that may be claiming too much.

The reality is that many good churches have been built upon the foundation of apostolic and prophetic writing in the scriptures, and without the help of living apostles and prophets. But apostles and prophets ministering today are also seen to be very effective in laying a good foundation for a body of believers. This is happening constantly with new church plantings in the Newfrontiers group of churches. It is probably right to see in this verse a reference to both living apostles and prophets as well as a reference to the apostolic and prophetic scriptures.

Prophets have a sensitivity that enables them to hear God. But because they are sensitive, they need to be given careful pastoral oversight. They look for approval and can be devastated by criticism. My wife tells me that prophets have a layer of skin missing! They can be lions on the platform on Sunday morning, but emotional wrecks on Monday morning. But that sensitivity does enable them to hear the Lord. It is important to listen to them, to weigh what they say, as the scripture suggests, and to feed back to them constructively.

A prophet can reawaken vision, give a specific direction to the vision and motivate people to fulfil the vision. It is very interesting to read in the Old Testament account that after the Exile the Temple was rebuilt with the help of the prophet Haggai. Prophets are foundation layers and builders; they stir God's people to action.

Experience would teach that it is probably best not to have a prophet leading the church. He can get so much revelation that the church can blow up trying to implement it all. It is not always wise to have elders who are prophets, for they tend to be impatient and frustrated when considering the small details of church life that elders must often give attention to. Discussing the need for a coach to pick up students from a nearby college to bring them to a Sunday meeting does not thrill a prophet!

Prophets can be so helpful when elders are stuck on a particular issue and they can ask the prophet to seek God for revelation.

Evangelists

The only named evangelist in the New Testament is Philip who had a particularly effective healing crusade in Samaria with the result that 'there was great joy in that city' (Acts 8:8). But Philip was also used by God to bring the Ethiopian eunuch to faith in Christ. Obviously whether he was speaking to crowds or witnessing to an individual, this New Testament evangelist had a passion to win people to Jesus.

The word 'evangelist' tends to bring a Billy Graham or a Luis Palau to our mind, but according to Ephesians 4 the ministry of the evangelist (together with all the other ministries) is to help equip the people of God for service (Ephesians 4:12).

An evangelist, therefore, is not only passionate himself to win people to faith, he will also have the ability to help the whole church have such a passion, and to equip the people of God for outreach. A gifted evangelist often travels among the churches, preaching the gospel and helping to equip different congregations in their evangelistic outreach.

Again, evangelists do not very often make the best elders. An evangelist leading a church can wear people out with constant exhortation to outreach. Also, if an evangelist is appointed as an elder he can become swamped with pastoral issues, rather than concentrating on his primary gift in winning the lost.

Pastor/teachers

Pastor/teachers are more commonly settled in one local church, but some will travel quite extensively, bringing their gift to various churches. Indeed sometimes a pastor/teacher will spend most of his time away from his own church ministering to other churches and leaders. When this happens he is likely to exercise definite pastoral care towards other leaders and to be used in a variety of teaching situations.

Now I am assuming here that pastor/teachers represent

two elements of one ministry rather than two separate ministries. For one thing Ephesians 4:11 reads like that. The ascended Christ gives some to be apostles, some to be prophets, some to be evangelists, and some to be pastors and teachers. Not some to be pastors and some to be teachers.

Rather more significantly, we need to understand the actual ministry here. Pastors are shepherds who desire to lead the sheep to good pasture where they will feed well. The best way to feed the flock of God is by teaching them the Word of God. On the other hand, teachers who bring people God's truth are really showing their care for people. There is a danger that if we separate the pastor and the teacher then we end up with pastors who are no more than visiting tea drinkers and teachers who are merely lecturers, dispensing truth to people for whom they have no active care.

Pastor/teachers will often be the elders of a local church and will oversee the church with care and stability. However, although they are committed to the maintenance of the church, and that is certainly not to be despised – my car won't even run if it is not maintained – they may lack the gifting to drive the church forward.

This is why we need the input of all the ministries for the health of a local church. The ascended Christ has given to the church, apostles, prophets, evangelists and pastors and teachers – all the ministries for all the churches.

Equipping ministries

Reading on from Ephesians 4:11 we see how these ministries help to equip the church.

They equip people to serve
'To prepare God's people for works of service' (v. 12). The apostle can motivate people to serve by planting a new church together. The prophet can stir us to corporate activity such as a new initiative in prayer. The evangelist will instruct us how

to serve in sharing the Gospel. The pastor/teacher will be able to explain the scriptures that make it clear everyone has a part to play in the body of Christ. He will also help individuals find their right place for serving in the church.

They help the church to be built up
'... so that the body of Christ may be built up' (v. 12). Some years ago the church where I am based purchased a warehouse (yes, we reversed the trend!), but we then had to work through a massive building programme which included putting a whole new floor and therefore a new roof onto the building.

The building was surrounded by scaffolding for months, which in turn was surrounded by a green gauze screen to protect the builders from the worst of weather. One Friday afternoon, the green gauze was removed and local office workers poured onto the streets to observe clearly for the first time that something had really been built. The ministries that the ascended Christ gives to the church can all contribute their gifts to help the people of God understand that they are really building a community of God together.

They encourage unity
'... until we all reach unity in the faith' (v. 13). I have often observed that apostles can draw different leaders together and cast a vision to get them all involved. I have seen Terry Virgo do this at many Bible Weeks and Leaders' Conferences.

Prophets can stir a passion for unity as they bring a sense of fresh revelation about this from the Lord.

Evangelists often succeed in helping believers from different churches and streams to work together in outreach. Pastor/teachers instruct people on reconciliation and forgiveness.

They bring the church to maturity
' ... and become mature' (v. 13). All of these ministries are helping the members of the church to become more like Christ. Although Paul was such a great apostle, we can appreciate his

pastoral concern when he writes, 'We proclaim him, admonishing and teaching everyone with all wisdom, so that we may present everyone perfect in Christ. To this end I labour, struggling with all his energy, which so powerfully works in me' (Colossians 1:28,29). He gave his best energies to help to bring God's people to maturity.

It is important that a church is making progress towards greater maturity, and all the different ministries can help here.

So these ministries that Christ gives are equipping ministries, helping the church to fulfil her vision and mission.

Positive results

If the church will receive the ministries that Christ gives to her, then very positive results will follow, as also indicated in Ephesians 4.

Stability
'Then we will no longer be infants, tossed back and forth by the waves, and blown here and there by every wind of teaching and by the cunning and craftiness of men in their deceitful scheming' (v. 14). There are a lot of storms around today, and plenty of wind and waves to blow the people of God off course. Individuals come with their agendas and can intimidate those who do not see things as they do. Television preachers promise us great prosperity while other preachers are calling us to a simple lifestyle.

The ministries that Christ gives, complementing one another and serving the local church, help to bring stability to the people of God.

Progress
'Instead, speaking the truth in love, we will in all things grow up into him who is the Head, that is, Christ' (v. 15).

In context, the 'truth' that is spoken of here is doctrinal

truth. A church that is well served by the different ministries will make progress in biblical understanding and the members will be able to minister the truth to one another. Speaking the truth in love is not about making your opinions known concerning another brother's dress sense. It is much more about strengthening your brother with God's truth in a time of crisis.

Fully functioning
'From him the whole body, joined and held together by every supporting ligament, grows and builds itself up in love, as each part does its work' (v. 16).

A church that accepts the ministries Christ gives, will be a church where every member is helped and encouraged to be fully functioning. When we all function together, we build one another up so that together we become a community that has the ability to astonish the world.

If the risen and ascended Christ has given these ministries to the church for her good, we are foolish if we refuse to receive them. Jesus promises a reward to those who will receive a prophet (Matthew 10:41). There is surely a principle here with regard to all these ministries. If we will receive these ministries then we will be rewarded. Indeed even though Christ gives these ministries, they can do us no good unless we receive them. But when a church does receive them it will bring a reward that will be seen in the church's progress.

Chapter 6   Leadership
Overseers of the flock

There is no shortage of books available on the subject of leadership and probably the ones we are most likely to take note of are those written by the pastors of today's megachurches around the world. If you lead the biggest church in the world, as Yongi Cho does, or if you lead one of the best attended churches in America, as Bill Hybels does, or if you pastor the fastest growing Baptist church in America, as Rick Warren does, then you can be sure these men have something worthwhile to communicate on the subject.

But most Christian leaders are not superstars and most local churches are not mega churches. So here I am simply stating that the Bible indicates that local churches are led by elders (sometimes called presbyters or bishops in the New Testament) and there seems no good reason to abandon this pattern of leadership. I am not really attempting here to describe how a leader can be more effective or more successful; there is plenty of help elsewhere for that, but rather what are the biblical principles for recognising and appointing leaders in the local church and how do they function?

At the time of writing this book I have had the privilege of serving with a team of elders in one church for some 18 years. For eight years I led the team before taking on a wider training and teaching role. One of the very distinctive features of our team has been its stability. Six of the eight elders have been together for all of those 18 years. One elder stepped down after some personal difficulties and two others have moved away to be involved in the leadership of other churches.

Working in such a long-term team, where relationships have almost always been excellent, enables me to write with some conviction and experience on this subject.

The New Testament always speaks of elders in the plural. The Bible recognises that it is not good for a man to be alone! Certainly where there are at least two elders then they can seek God together and watch over one another in leadership. God raises an elder up, so occasionally we have to wait for other elders to be raised up – we cannot rush ahead of God. But in Titus 1:5 Paul tells Titus to appoint elders in every church.

It will be seen that Paul's most common way of starting a letter is to address the 'saints', referring to the whole church. This should certainly stop elders getting an over inflated sense of position. However, at the beginning of his letter to the Philippians Paul does address the 'overseers' (or elders) and in Acts 14 Paul and Barnabas appointed elders in each church that they visited. There are various other references to elders in Acts where they are always referred to in the plural.

The spirit of New Testament leadership

It is very clear from the Bible that the spirit of leadership is to be in the nature of servant leadership. There is never a hint of leadership being established to manipulate or control others, to create a climate of fear or to be regarded as elevated or distant. Christ himself sets the pattern, 'For even the Son of Man did not come to be served, but to serve, and to give his life as a ransom for many' (Mark 10:45). Even the wonderful description of the descent and ascent of Christ given in Philippians 2 is written to challenge us about servanthood. 'Your attitude should be the same as that of Christ Jesus' (Philippians 2:5). Indeed to serve us and to give his life for us, Christ descended from the highest place in glory to the lowest form of death, being crucified at Calvary. No one was more exalted than Jesus and no one more humbled himself to win a people, than Jesus. This needs to be remembered by every leader in the church of Jesus Christ.

In John 10 we read of Jesus as the good shepherd who lays down his life for the sheep. Elders are under-shepherds (sometimes called shepherds) who are to care for the sheep and with a willingness to lay down their life for the sheep. We can get into total unreality here. Christ did actually die for us but it is highly unlikely that an elder today will have to do that in western society. It is easy to feel that talk of laying down our life is a nice spiritual thought but in a way totally irrelevant.

However an elder needs to think in terms of giving his life for people. He can do this in giving his time and energy and working hard on their behalf. Even for a so-called full-time elder we are not talking of a career, but of a call from God to serve a people. This is emphasised in 1 Peter 5 where an elder is described as someone willing to serve and not lording it over those entrusted to him. 'Entrust' is a big word; it really speaks of a serious responsibility to care for people, certainly not to boss or control them. So the spirit of leadership is to be that of self-giving love to serve others.

Character qualifications of elders

In the New Testament elders are not those with charm or charisma, though these could be helpful. Rather, they are men whose good characters are evident and can be described. We are helped to identify such men in 1 Timothy 3:1–7.

From those verses we see that elders are to be:

Above reproach. In general terms this is speaking of men of good character. Typically Paul starts here with a general statement before moving on to the detail.

The husband of one wife. This has been variously interpreted over the years. For example in the Orthodox churches a priest cannot remarry even if his wife dies – he can have only one wife. It could be understood in certain societies to mean a monogamous marriage. We should probably see here a wider reference to a secure marriage. An elder needs the support of his wife for his ministry, without which support her husband's ministry can be wrecked, but this does not mean that an elder's wife has to have her own recognised ministry.

Temperate. I once served on a leadership team where one of the other members could only be described as a dormant volcano. The fear was that at any time he might blow! The result was that the rest of the team was always nervous to talk about certain subjects in case the volcano erupted. Elders need to be able to express their opinions, but to do so in a reasonable and non-threatening manner.

Respectable. This sounds a rather old-fashioned term, but could have reference to the way an elder dresses, personal habits and speech. An elder who wears dirty clothes, smokes and swears is not liable to gain much of a following – at least not in the church!

Hospitable. This is important not only for the elder to have the opportunity to know his people, but so his people can know him in his home setting and are able to observe what he is really like!

Able to teach. An elder must be able to communicate effectively the truth of God to others. This does not however mean he necessarily has to do this from a pulpit or platform. 1 Timothy 5:17 speaks of those elders whose work is preaching and teaching, which seems to imply that for some elders this is not their main ministry. However every elder must be able to teach others at some level or he cannot properly care for his people.

Not given to drunkenness. Despite what some Christians have tried to force onto the Bible there are no texts that require believers to be teetotal, though some may choose that to be their personal commitment. However the Bible registers a total opposition to believers drinking too much and obviously elders need to set a good example here.

Not violent but gentle. An elder should not be the kind of man that causes others to be afraid of him. He should be approachable and open-hearted.

Not quarrelsome. An elder must not be a person looking for a fight. It is important that issues and even people are confronted when there is sin, or when there is behaviour or attitudes that could damage the body of Christ. But an elder is not to be one who delights in confrontations.

Not a lover of money. The three greatest temptations that face leaders are to do with money, sex and power. It can be assumed that the leaders facing the strongest sexual temptations will be the younger men. In practice I have found that leaders in their 40s and 50s are the ones who have most often wrecked their ministries by falling into sin, especially sexual sin.

There is a temptation to those with spiritual authority to use it for spiritual abuse and control of others. Money can be a temptation to a leader at any time and Peter also warns elders not to be greedy for money (1 Peter 5.2).

A good manager of his own family. This is plain common sense. How can a man exercise government in the church if there is no sense of order in his family? I have known this to be a big issue for some elders whose children are going through difficult times. There is a need here to be realistic and not legalistic. Small children will stick their tongues out and teenagers often go through rebellious periods. But clearly there can be occasions when family difficulties are extreme enough for it to be inappropriate for a man to continue as an elder. He may need the time and space to give greater attention to his family.

Not a recent convert. It is simply good advice not to appoint a person too quickly to a place of spiritual authority. Such evidence as we have in the New Testament would suggest that elders were not appointed immediately a church was planted; time was given to see whom God was raising up to leadership.

A good reputation with outsiders. If a neighbour knows this man is beating his wife then that is not a good qualification for eldership. Even if the neighbour doesn't know, it is still not a good qualification!

I do know of one church where the leader asked for a

reference from a prospective elder's employer before appointing him. It was a serious attempt to check that someone about to be appointed as an elder in the church did have a good reputation with outsiders.

How does an elder function?

Paul's farewell to the Ephesian elders is particularly helpful in giving to us an understanding of the ministry of these leaders. Paul stayed in Ephesus for about three years and this was probably his most fruitful time of ministry.

Some time later on his way back to Jerusalem from another missionary trip, and aware that prison and hardships were ahead, he passed through Ephesus. This gave him the opportunity to meet with the elders of the church there once more and to give them some final instructions. There was great sadness at this meeting, resulting from the huge affection between Paul and these elders and the assumption that they would never see each other again. Paul says to them, 'Keep watch over yourselves and all the flock of which the Holy Spirit has made you overseers. Be shepherds of the church of God, which he bought with his own blood' (Acts 20:28). Paul's final words to the elders of the church that he had invested most time into, must give a key insight into the way that elders are to function.

Keep a guard on yourself. This simply makes the point that we cannot lead others if we have not learned the disciplines of keeping our own life in good order.

Keep watch over the flock. Elders are to keep a sharp lookout for the people of God. Later on Paul talks of savage wolves that will come in and do damage to the flock. There is a need to teach, encourage and care for the people of God. Just as sheep can be silly, so immature believers can sometimes do some fairly stupid things. I have known believers who have got into a spat in the church, which has ended with punches being thrown! This is not a common feature of church life, but does indicate that there are some sheep that need a lot of help.

However immature the sheep, the shepherd does not despise or mock them; he gives his attention to looking after them. In these days of 24-hour Christian television there is the danger of individual believers regarding the superstar preachers on screen as their pastors. But these men do not know you and, while their preaching may inspire you, they cannot personally watch out for you and care for you.

Overseers. To be an overseer means that an elder gives direction to the flock. Elders should be able to discern the will of God for the church and get a sense of direction as to where this church needs to go. They are able to say, 'this is the way' and expect to be followed.

Over the years I have been able to observe how elders come to decisions together. Most commonly it is by consensus; the elders talk an issue through and come to an agreement.

If there is no consensus then sometimes the answer comes by revelation. On one occasion when I was leading the team of elders in our church in Brighton we needed to make a decision about the next phase of a huge building programme. The costs had escalated alarmingly and we were finding it difficult to come to the decision together as to whether we should proceed. I suggested that we all took a walk and sought God on our own. Very quickly I found that God was speaking to me about preaching a vision for the future rather than worrying about the costs.

When I brought this back to the elders an hour later it was felt that we had received a revelation from God on this issue and could move forward with confidence. We did and raised more than another million pounds!

If there is no consensus and no revelation then a decision has to be reached by authority and submission. This is one practical reason for having a lead elder. There are some occasions when he will have to say, 'This is what we will do,' and it will then be the responsibility of the other elders to submit to that. In a good team this works well.

Shepherds. As soon as Paul has said 'overseers' with the

emphasis being on giving direction, he reminds them again that they are shepherds. Elders do not bully people; even though they give direction, they also are to care passionately for the people of God. They therefore lead the people and do not drive them.

The reality is that leaders come and go. Very often they go for good reasons, like moving on to plant a new church. Sometimes they go for natural reasons like retirement. A few have to go for bad reasons. But the church is always being built. I remember once hearing C.J. Mahaney, who was then leading a very large church in the USA, say, 'I am only keeping the seat in my office warm for my successor.' It's difficult for elders to avoid talking about 'my church' because they have a care for a particular group of people, but it must never be *my* church; for the church is Christ's, purchased with his blood. Elders must always remember that.

Genuine leadership

In 1 Timothy 5:17 there is a reference to elders directing the affairs of the church and so although such leadership is to be servant leadership it is to be genuine leadership. Churches are fortunate when they have elders who oversee well, giving good teaching, good care, and good direction, and who effectively communicate a sense of purpose.

The same scripture says that elders who do well are worthy of 'double honour'. Certainly this could be a reference to money, although it can conjure up a picture of some management board or a similar group sitting down to discuss the performance of a particular elder and awarding a greater or lesser pay rise as a result. It is hard to conceive that this was really in Paul's mind.

There is certainly enough in the text and context to indicate that this might be referring to money although it may simply be a reference to an elder being 'highly regarded'. I minister in a church where the desire has always been to pay the elders a fair average wage, and not to deliberately keep the leaders poor for the purpose of their sanctification!

We moved away from a rather haphazard system of determining salaries in our church some years ago and placed everyone on a professional salary scale. This at least made salaries relate to what many of our members are being paid and brought a degree of objectivity.

I sometimes put it this way: elders should be paid enough not to have to worry, but not enough to fly Business Class. I appreciate that some sections of the church would probably teach that only First Class is appropriate, but then others would question the need to fly at all!

Receiving oversight

Churches need leaders so as to avoid chaos, stagnation and anarchy. They need God-given leaders. The New Testament also teaches leadership in marriage, in the family and at work as well as in the church. God desires that relationships work properly and one vital key to that is good leadership.

In the church, elders are to be received, respected and obeyed (Hebrews 13:17). The reference to obedience is a challenging concept in a society increasingly given to ignoring and even despising authority. Obedience to leaders is to be given in regard to the Word of God. If a leader tells us not to gossip, then that comes with biblical authority. But if a leader tells us not to keep a cat at home then a polite 'mind your own business' would not be inappropriate as there is no biblical authority for that.

Of course, advice is different. If asked, a leader may have a very good reason for suggesting that it's not a good idea to keep a cat at home (say, one of the family is prone to asthma). But that is different, for advice can be listened to but disregarded.

A risk

If we follow a man there is always a risk. We cannot avoid this painful truth. Three kings arose in Israel's early history and all were charismatic and dynamic leaders. One was called Saul, another David and the third was Absalom. Only one of them was worth following and he had his weaknesses.

There is always a risk in following a man. But with elders there are ways to minimise this risk. To have more than one elder obviously helps. Also to welcome other travelling ministries that visit from time to time is helpful here.

God raises up elders in the church. They are to be men of good character, in line with what has already been described, and though giving oversight and leadership, are to have a servant heart.

The people of God can follow such leaders with faith and confidence.

Chapter 7   Grace
Lavish and undeserved

Some years ago I was about to board an Emirates flight from Mumbai in India to Dubai. I fly very regularly, but I had never previously been upgraded to Business Class. On this occasion, however, as I queued for the plane I was unexpectedly pulled out of the line by a flight official and given a Business Class ticket.

Emirates are one of the world's best airlines and I was soon enjoying the comfortable seat, an amazing amount of space in which to stretch out, and excellent food.

A steward came round and gave us all a present packed in a small box. I opened it up to discover that I had been given a crystal glass cat, one of six animal figurines that were being given out as souvenirs of the flight. I put it in the pocket in front of me smugly satisfied with what would be a future reminder of travelling Business Class.

An elderly Indian lady sitting next to me nudged me and pointed to the pocket containing my glass cat. I assumed that she wanted to see what animal I had been given – I hadn't seen which one she'd received. I willingly gave her mine to look at. She opened her handbag, dropped it in and shut the bag!

I was outraged! I couldn't shake her and point to my cat – she was too old and frail. I couldn't speak to her, and demand my cat back, as she didn't understand English. So I just sat and fumed, outraged at the loss of my little glass cat.

Then God began to speak to me about grace!

I found myself acknowledging that I hadn't paid for the Business Class seat, I didn't deserve it, I had just been pulled out of the line and freely given the seat. So why was I so upset about the loss of a little glass cat?

We have done nothing to deserve our salvation. We haven't paid for our salvation. God, in his grace, pulled us out of the line and freely gave us salvation. In view of God's grace towards us why do we so often get so upset at a little loss or inconvenience in our lives?

The word 'grace' can very easily trip off the tongues of Christians, but what is it?

It is certainly not some impersonal force, but indicates the attitude of God towards us. Sometimes grace has been defined as God's Riches At Christ's Expense and certainly this indicates that we have received from God rather than the idea that we have given something to God, or even that we deserve something from him.

Whereas the mercy of God means that we have not received what we deserve, the grace of God means that we have received what we do not deserve. Grace is the undeserved favour of God towards us. There is a deposit of divine energy in our lives that has brought us out of spiritual death and continues to manifest the favour of God in us.

Interpretation

One passage in the New Testament that really helps us to appreciate God's grace is also one of the most controversial and that is in Romans 7.

Among evangelical Christians there is a great amount of agreement about our understanding of the Bible. The advent of the charismatic movement caused many to look again at the scriptures that speak about spiritual gifts. More and more evangelical Christians have accepted that there are spiritual gifts for the church today, and that they did not all die out after the apostolic era. It has not been a matter of charismatics winning a vote on the matter, or being persuasive because they are often more lively in a church meeting! It has come down to the issue of what the Bible is really and clearly saying on this matter.

But there are a few passages in the New Testament that still cause wide-ranging debates. One of these is Revelation 20 with its description of the thousand-year reign of Christ. In trying to decide what really drives our interpretation of a passage like this we may find it involves a number of factors such as a mixture of previously held convictions, the views of certain well-known Bible teachers, and perhaps even something of our own temperament and preferences.

The same can possibly be said about Romans 7:7–25. Many Christians are persuaded that Paul is speaking about a believer's experience here. But other Christians are convinced that this is the testimony of an unconverted man who can only find his answer in Christ. Is this man a Christian, or not a Christian? There is no universal agreement among evangelical believers. But again why do we make our decision here? Does it have a lot to do with our own personality or temperament? Here are some brief points on both sides of the argument.

Some say the man is a Christian

1. Paul uses personal pronouns, 'I', 'me', or 'my', forty times in this passage. It is written in the present tense all the way through e.g. 'What a wretched man I am!' (v. 24). So Paul is speaking of his present experience as a Christian.

2. Paul speaks of the Law as only a Christian would. He refers to it as spiritual, good and delightful.

3. Elsewhere in the New Testament Paul speaks of the 'inner being' or the 'inner person' only when referring to a Christian. Paul does that again here in verse 22: 'For in my inner being I delight in God's law'. So, this refers to Paul as the Christian.

4. Then consider verse 25. 'Thanks be to God – through Jesus Christ our Lord! So then, I myself in my mind am a slave

to God's law, but in the sinful nature a slave to the law of sin.' Paul begins the verse by speaking of the deliverance that is his in Christ and he finishes by talking of the struggle he is going through. This is true Christian experience. A believer is one delivered by Christ, but still struggling with the issue of obedience to the Law and with sin still a present reality.

Many Christians would say that Romans 7 describes true Christian experience and one they can identify with.

But others say this man is not a Christian

1. Paul uses the term 'flesh'. E.g. verse 18: 'I know that nothing good lives ... in my flesh', (not 'sinful nature' as in the New International Version), and this is the term he uses in the New Testament for the unconverted.
2. Paul says, 'We know that the Law is spiritual; but I am unspiritual, sold as a slave to sin' (v. 14). The claim is that this cannot possibly describe a Christian because in Romans 6:11, Paul has said: 'In the same way, count yourselves dead to sin but alive to God in Christ Jesus.' Therefore, Paul has stated already that a Christian is in exactly the opposite situation to that described here in Romans 7.
3. Again, we read, 'but I see another law at work in the members of my body, waging war against the law of my mind and making me a prisoner of the law of sin at work within my members' (v. 23). But how could Paul describe a Christian as a prisoner of the law of sin when in Romans 8:2 he goes on to say that the believer is set free from the law of sin? So he is describing an unbeliever here in chapter 7.
4. A Christian may have his struggles with sin; but this passage speaks of a man defeated by sin and overwhelmed with failure.

So now we have strong arguments for saying that this man is not a believer.

How do we decide on the right interpretation? Perhaps we really make our decision according to our personality! I have noticed generally that those who believe the man of Romans 7 is a Christian tend to be introverts: they read their own experience into the passage. Generally, those who believe the man is not a Christian tend to be extroverts and optimists. Their Christian experience does not seem so much like this.

Fortunately we can interpret it either way without falling into heresy! We can certainly be wrong on our interpretation of one passage of scripture, but still right in our view of the Christian life as a whole.

So, those who say that the man of Romans 7 is not a Christian can still accept that sometimes Christians do have experiences like this when they feel pretty wretched about themselves. On the other hand, those who think the man of Romans 7 is a Christian can still believe that much more victory over sin is possible for the believer.

Where is Paul going?

Why does Paul introduce the subject of this wretched man (v. 24) at this stage of his letter? We need to see it in the context of his whole continuing argument.

Paul begins this epistle by spelling out the universal and total sinfulness of all mankind. However God has intervened with the gospel of grace. There is now an alternative way of righteousness provided for men and women. There is a God-given righteousness that we receive by faith. 'But now a righteousness from God, apart from law, has been made known, to which the Law and the Prophets testify. This righteousness from God comes through faith in Jesus Christ' (Romans 3:21,22). This is imputed or God-given righteousness and Paul speaks of this through Romans 3 and 4 stressing that this declaration of our righteousness is not achieved by works of the law nor by our own efforts.

In Romans 7 Paul indicates that the law really creates a problem for us, but he also makes this dramatic statement, 'So, my brothers, you also died to the law through the body of Christ, that you might belong to another, to him who was raised from the dead, in order that we might bear fruit to God' (Romans 7:4).

This potentially raises a big question, especially for the Jews – is Paul saying that there is something wrong with the law itself? Paul denies this: 'What shall we say, then? Is the law sin? Certainly not!' (Romans 7:7), and again: 'Did that which is good (the law), then, become death to me? By no means!' (Romans 7:13).

Paul goes to some lengths to make it clear that there is nothing wrong with the law itself. Indeed the law is good. The problem is with us. We break the law and that is why we must have Christ. The law cannot do for us what only Christ can do for us. Paul makes it very plain that the problem is with us and not with the law itself. 'We know that the law is spiritual; but I am unspiritual, sold as a slave to sin' (7:14). 'And if I do what I do not want to do, I agree that the law is good' (7:16). But although the law is spiritual and good it is powerless to justify us. Therefore the glorious truth of the gospel in exalting the work of Christ for our salvation still stands.

But Paul is dealing with the fact that the law creates a problem for us. The law itself is good, and we are sinful, and the law does not have the power to save us.

Amazing grace

At this point I believe we need to understand that if all our focus is on whether the man in Romans 7 is a Christian or not a Christian then we have lost the plot.

Having talked of the sinfulness of man, imputed right-eousness through faith in Christ and our problem with the law, which is good, Paul still needs to tackle a particular issue. Individuals insist on trying to get right with God through the law; they attempt to attain righteousness themselves.

So Paul is stressing that the law is good, but a man finds that in fact he cannot live up to it: 'I am unspiritual, sold as a slave to sin. I do not understand what I do. For what I want to do I do not do, but what I hate I do' (7:14,15). In other words the problem here is one of legalism, which is the very opposite to grace. It is the difficulty faced by someone who recognises the goodness of God's law, and he wants to live it out, but fails to do so.

The real issue is not whether this man is a Christian or not a Christian, but rather that he is a person seeking to get right with God through works of the law. There are non-Christians like this. They see the Ten Commandments as good, or they view the Sermon on the Mount as the right way to live. They may even make New Year resolutions on how to live in the coming year. In some way they recognise or set up a law as the way to live. But they fail to live out what they believe to be right and so feel wretched and condemned.

But there are true Christians like this as well. They trust in Christ alone for salvation, but then begin to see their own holiness as the way to win God's favour. Failures in holiness could mean losing the favour of God, indeed even losing their salvation. So the Christian, or the non-Christian, can end up crying out, 'What a wretched man I am!' Legalism does that to people – it makes them worriers, they feel wretched about themselves and constant failures.

But right through Romans, Paul has been arguing that through the grace of God justification is by faith. He is arguing that again now in the face of legalism.

What is the answer to legalism? Jesus Christ is the only answer to legalism: 'What a wretched man I am! Who will deliver me from this body of death?' (7:24). But here comes the answer: 'Thanks be to God – through Jesus Christ our Lord!'

(7:25). So we are saved and continue to be saved, by Christ, and not through the works of the law.

Romans 7 tells us precisely what our relationship to the law is, when we are 'in Christ'.

> *So, my brothers, you also died to the law through the body of Christ, that you might belong to another, to him who was raised from the dead, in order that we might bear fruit to God (7:4).*

In Christ we have died to the law. This is not saying the law has died, and we simply scrap it. Rather, we have died to the law as the way of getting right with God. We do not get right with God through the law, but by being 'in Christ'.

The Christian life

But we have also died to the law in terms of how we live the Christian life. There is a common view that although the law cannot justify us, we will be sanctified by the law. In other words, having become Christians we now live out our Christian life by being obedient to the law. What is the result of this approach? Quite simply that we are back under the law. But Romans 7:4 has told us that the way we bear fruit for God is not by living out the law, but rather by living out our relationship with Christ.

Again, Paul says: 'But now, by dying to what once bound us, we have been released from the law so that we serve in the new way of the Spirit, and not in the old way of the written code' (7:6). As believers we have died to the law and so it is clear that we are not meant to go back to it. We do not serve God by the old way of the written code; now we serve God in a new way, by the Spirit.

For the Christian the Holy Spirit has replaced the law. So, we now live in Christ, and Christ lives in us. This is life in the Spirit, and therefore a life that should more and more demonstrate and represent Christ.

The point may be raised about Christ himself perfectly fulfilling the law. But if we live our life in Christ, we will fulfil the law automatically. It will not be because we are serving the law, but because we are living for Christ.

Legalists can feel that if they fail to read their Bible in a particular way or even at a particular time then God will not love them. The Christian who understands grace does not say, I won't read my Bible because it doesn't matter, God will still love me. He discovers that the Spirit within him creates a desire to read the Word of God. This still takes discipline, but it is a response to the leading of the Spirit in his life.

Take the situation of a man who has read pornographic magazines before he was converted. He believes in Christ and knows that God declares him righteous. The magazines he used to look at still continue to be printed and sold, and he still has a pair of eyes that can look at them. What now causes him to read Christian books rather than pornographic magazines? It is the desire created in him by the Spirit to live like Christ. In fact, living like Christ will always take us beyond the law. The law sets a minimum; living for Christ is abundant life, it is the maximum.

Having laid down these principles of our dying to the law and serving in the new way of the Spirit, this is what Paul then brings us back to at the end of chapter 7. For the non-believer who might say, as he looks at his life, what a wretched man I am, or, for the believer who is struggling with legalism and condemnation and crying out, what a wretched man I am, there is an answer: 'Thanks be to God – through Jesus Christ our Lord!'

As Paul says in Romans 8: 'You, however, are controlled not by the sinful nature but by the Spirit, if the Spirit of God lives in you' (v. 9).

We must resist the tendency to be drawn back into legalism. The church is actually a community of grace led by the Spirit of God. That is what we are able to demonstrate.

Chapter 8   # Water
Death, burial, resurrection and celebration

Years ago, I knew a Baptist pastor who was friends with an Anglican vicar in the same town. The vicar had become convinced of the rightness of baptising believers by total immersion. As this was something he had never previously done, he sought advice from the Baptist. The Baptist minister explained the practical details as well as he could and met up with his Anglican friend a few days after the service had taken place.

Naturally, the Baptist pastor was eager to know how the service had gone in his friend's church. 'We had a great time,' said the vicar, 'but do you find that your candidates get very short of breath when you baptise them?' The Baptist was puzzled and pressed for details. 'I did as you said,' replied the vicar. 'I put them under the water and said, "I baptise you in the name of God the Father, God the Son and God the Holy Spirit. Amen" but when they came up out of the water they were gasping for breath!'

It is true that at one level, baptism is reminding us of a death and a burial. But because this is Christian baptism, we are also being reminded of resurrection. Every candidate who is buried in the waters of baptism surfaces again in celebration of the resurrection to eternal life.

Romans 6

Or don't you know that all of us who were baptised into Christ Jesus were baptised into his death? We were therefore buried

77

> *with him through baptism into death in order that, just as Christ*
> *was raised from the dead through the glory of the Father, we too*
> *may live a new life (Romans 6:3,4).*

It is very easy to read this Scripture as though it is speaking directly of water baptism. I doubt this.

If we go to the book of Ephesians we read there of 'one body and one Spirit – just as you were called to one hope when you were called – one Lord, one faith, one baptism; one God and Father of all ...' (Ephesians 4:4–6). The seven 'ones' that are mentioned here are a vital key to our unity for they speak of matters that are true for all believers.

However, there is a particular challenge when we read of 'one baptism'. Here staunchly evangelical Christians seem widely separated. Some are baptised as babies, some are baptised as believers and some are not baptised at all. Some have been sprinkled with water and others have been fully immersed. So how can we speak of one baptism?

The answer is found in Romans 6:3 and in the reference to being baptised into Christ. All Christians have been baptised or placed into Christ. Indeed 'in Christ' is Paul's favourite term for the Christian.

There would certainly be a secondary reference to water baptism in Romans 6, in the sense that baptism in water is a picture of what has happened in our lives by our being baptised into Christ.

Taking the reference in Romans 6 to baptism into Christ as being baptised into Christ's death and being raised to new life in him, it is hardly difficult to understand the symbolism of water baptism. To be placed under the water represents our death and burial in Christ. To be raised up out of the water represents our resurrection to new life and eternal life in Jesus Christ. Such symbolism indicates why baptism by total immersion is the best way of doing it, with its dramatic picture of burial and resurrection.

Over the years I have had many conversations with

evangelical Christians who follow the practice of infant baptism. By the way, the comparison here is not between infant baptism and adult baptism, but between the baptism of babies who have obviously made no declaration of faith and baptism of believers, irrespective of age.

In such conversations I have always understood there is a reasonable argument that can be made for infant baptism. Often a parallel is drawn with the circumcision of Jewish males when they were just a few days old as a mark of their belonging to the covenant community of God. Baptism is a mark of belonging to the covenant people of God today.

However, everyone born into Israel in the time of the old covenant was born into God's nation. But today anyone only comes into God's nation by being born again.

Anyway, why make life complicated? Why don't we just follow the clear New Testament pattern? There is no occasion of baptism being described in the New Testament when it was not clearly for believers. The rather feeble suggestion that the jailer's household at Philippi who were baptised by Paul must have included babies is not even an argument from silence. We read: 'he (the jailer) was filled with joy because he had come to believe in God – he and his whole family' (Acts 16:34). Everyone in that family was baptised because everyone believed.

Bearing in mind the symbolism of baptism and the fact that in the New Testament every person who is baptised is clearly a Christian, it seems unfortunate to say the least that Christians who are agreed on the gospel continue to maintain different practices with water baptism.

Too much?

I think it is possible to put too much emphasis on baptism with the result that we can become over-concerned about certain details. One of the questions that comes up is how soon should we baptise someone after they have confessed Christ?

We can certainly make out a case from the New Testament

for immediate baptism. The 3,000 who were converted on the day of Pentecost were baptised immediately they believed, and so was the Ethiopian eunuch, and so were the Philippian jailer and his family.

There even seem to be scriptures that link conversion and baptism together (1 Peter 3:21).

Yet, as we study the history of the early church, we find that candidates for baptism went through a long period of instruction before their baptism. The risk with instant baptism is obviously that the person may not have been genuinely converted. Indeed I have known pastors who believe they have seen a biblical case for baptising immediately faith is confessed, but who have quickly abandoned it in practice when none of the 'converts' were found to continue in the faith.

On the other hand, we can hold people back from baptism as we look for what we feel is an acceptable standard of behaviour for them to be regarded as suitable candidates. What we can then be doing is baptising people as a demonstration of their sanctification, when clearly in the Bible it is a picture of their justification.

This also touches a further issue about the age of those who should be baptised. Bearing in mind that the New Testament pattern is clearly believers' baptism, how young can a believer be when he or she is baptised? I have known churches that have established a 'rule' that no one can be baptised before the age of 16.

Again, we face a couple of risks here. If we baptise young children can we be sure that they are true believers and could there even be the possibility that some children want to be baptised because that is what their friends are doing? On the other hand, if we make a rule about age, we can again be baptising people for sanctification rather than for justification.

In practice, we can find that someone baptised as a young child goes on steadily in the faith, whereas an adult fails to stand even after a delay in baptising him or her in our desire to try and be certain of his or her faith. I was baptised at the age of fifteen with a group of eight other young people all about the same age, after several weeks of instruction. I married one of the eight who I know continues in the faith! But the other seven quickly drifted right away from God. If we put too much emphasis on getting this right we are soon going to find out that in a number of instances we can get it wrong.

Leaders have to lead and show wisdom and discernment. The best way forward would seem to be that, having an absolute principle that baptism is for believers, then we baptise believers as soon as it is reasonably possible. We look for clear indication of saving faith and basically we have to accept people as they present themselves to us. If children want to be baptised we obviously involve the parents in the decision. What we need to avoid is a casual approach to baptism, which makes it so instant that the candidate is not really checked out at all.

We also need to avoid waiting for some level of sanctification that we feel is appropriate and forgetting that baptism actually demonstrates our death and resurrection in Christ when we begin our Christian life.

I realise that the biblical challenge seems to come with regard to the Day of Pentecost particularly. Surely, this could be regarded as somewhat casual with 3,000 being instantly baptised – the disciples would not have been able to check out all those people. But we need to remember that these were Jews who were responding and that they already believed in God and moreover had an understanding of baptism because converts to Judaism were also baptised. These were not pagans, but believers in God who were now fully embracing the truth of Christ as their Messiah. We may need to take a little more care when people come in from a totally non-faith background.

It is also possible that too much emphasis can be wrongly placed on the baptismal service. We can see such an occasion as bait to hook the unbeliever rather than an event that celebrates the new life that believers now have. In fact in the New

Testament new believers were not always baptised publicly. There were no leaflets inviting people to come and watch the Ethiopian eunuch being baptised or the Philippian jailer or the twelve men at Ephesus.

Obviously, testimonies that are given at a time of baptism can be very encouraging for the church and sometimes convicting for unbelievers who may be present. The baptism itself is a picture demonstration of the gospel, but we must take care not to put so much emphasis on the outreach side of the occasion that we fail to put sufficient focus on the joy of celebrating the believer's salvation.

Too little

In another way, it is possible to put too little emphasis on baptism. Here again, Paul's teaching in Romans 6 is very helpful. Romans 6 has a lot to say about the Christian's victory over sin. The beginning of the chapter immediately calls our attention to this. 'What shall we say, then? Shall we go on sinning, so that grace may increase? By no means! We died to sin; how can we live in it any longer?' (Romans 6:1,2). A crucial verse is reached halfway through the chapter when Paul issues his first instruction in this letter. 'In the same way, count yourselves dead to sin but alive to God in Christ Jesus' (Romans 6:11). So we find that Paul is teaching us about victory over sin in this important chapter.

Again, we need to remind ourselves that this chapter speaks of a baptism into Christ (v. 3). Water baptism is a picture of this baptism into Christ; speaking of the fact that we have died to our old life and been raised to new life. When we have been baptised in water there can be, I suggest, the real danger that we then regard it too lightly.

How often do we think back to the time of our baptism? We are engaged in a battle against sin, how do we overcome? Well, here is one way; we recall our baptism. We remind ourselves that we were once immersed in water – a vital picture and demonstration of what is most true and important for me. I am a person 'in Christ' – what does that mean? Well, for one thing it means that I have died to my old life of sin and rebellion against God. I've shown that in my funeral service. My baptism was a far more important funeral service than the one that I shall have in the future. The funeral service to come will be a goodbye to this old body. But in baptism, my old life has already been buried.

In baptism there was a picture and testimony to the fact that I had died to my old pre-Christian life. But Jesus Christ was raised from the dead. Because I am 'in Christ' I am also raised from the dead. As I came up out of the water, there was a living demonstration of this truth as well. I am alive 'in Christ'. I shall live forever because Christ lives forever.

To recall these truths helps us to gain the victory in our battle against sin. To remember our baptism is to remember that the truth of who I am 'in Christ' has been vitally demonstrated and proclaimed. I didn't just get wet. I wasn't just part of an evangelistic guest service. Rather I proclaimed I had died, and had also been raised to life 'in Christ'.

Too little can be made of our baptism when in reality it can be a lifelong help in gaining victory over sin.

Rebaptism?

This can be an awkward issue between churches that practice infant baptism and those churches that baptise believers. I have known numerous cases of individuals asking for believers' baptism that has caused real pain back at the church where the person previously attended or real pain in their family.

It can become particularly critical in the case of, say, a student who has previously been a member of an Anglican Church and comes from a believing family that is still worshipping at that church. Arriving at university and starting to attend a church that teaches believers' baptism, the student now wishes to be baptised as a believer. The cry from the home church and from the family is that he or she surely cannot be rebaptised – they have already been baptised, as a baby.

I would agree that a rebaptism should not take place. There is no indication of such a possibility in the New Testament. If it is suggested that this is an argument from silence we would have to say it is a clear theological issue. We are only justified once and if baptism is a picture of that, then we can only be baptised once. So the issue here is not in fact about 'rebaptism'; rather there is the conviction that making a baby wet does not baptise them. In the New Testament only believers were baptised. So whatever has preceded believers' baptism is not the New Testament way and therefore believers' baptism is not a rebaptism.

Let me play out an unlikely, but not totally impossible scenario. As a small baby, Tom is christened at the local Anglican Church. As a teenager he responds to a visitor at his door one day with the result that he joins a local Kingdom Hall of Jehovah's Witnesses. He is now a believer in their doctrine and is baptised in water to become a full member of their group.

At the age of 24 Tom meets and falls in love with a young lady at his office who is a Mormon. Not surprisingly, he wants to know what she believes and you've guessed it – before they are married, he embraces her beliefs. He is now baptised into the Mormon Church. Discovering 23 dead relatives in his family line, and following Mormon doctrine on an obscure text in 1 Corinthians 15 about baptism on behalf of the dead, he goes along with Mormon practice and is baptised another 23 times on behalf of those dead relatives.

So Tom has already been 'baptised' 26 times by the time he and his wife are invited to attend an Alpha Course at the local Baptist Church. Tom is then truly converted, and yes he is baptised again. Except that he is not actually baptised again, he is baptised for the first time. On all previous 26 occasions, he got wet, but now he is baptised as a believer in Christ, this being the only baptism that the New Testament recognises. Only this baptism can demonstrate death to the old life and resurrection to new life in Christ.

Which method?

What about the person who became a true Christian after beginning to attend an Anglican Church and was baptised therefore as a believer at, say, the age of 20? When this happens the person is usually sprinkled with water (affusion), not placed under the water (immersion). Here we must distinguish between believers' baptism, which is primary and the mode of baptism, which is secondary.

Total immersion is clearly the best method for baptism because it makes the symbolism of death and resurrection so clear. However, if a person is baptised as a believer, by having water sprinkled on them, then to baptise them again by a better method with more water would be to make the secondary primary and would really be a rebaptism. That should not be done.

This also applies when a person claims that they didn't understand the meaning of their baptism and asks, 'Can I be done again?' The issue here is whether they were believers when they were baptised. If they were to be immersed again simply because they now have a fuller understanding then this would be a rebaptism. Rather they need instruction from Romans 6 so that they can now look back on their baptism with understanding.

Jesus said, 'Therefore go and make disciples of all nations, baptising them in the name of the Father and of the Son and of the Holy Spirit' (Matthew 28:19).

In seeking the restoration of the church to a true biblical pattern on the issue of water baptism, why complicate it? Why not just do what Jesus said?

Chapter 9   **Fire**
Baptised by the Spirit

I have been in Christian ministry long enough to remember some of the first stirrings of the charismatic movement that took place during the time that I was a student at a Baptist Training College in London (1965–69). For a short time I aligned myself with a small group in the college who were definitely seeking more of the Holy Spirit's influence in their lives. There was zeal combined with perhaps limited maturity, but it was my first contact with anything charismatic. At the same time, there was news of new moves of God in several places. Some extraordinary happenings were being reported from a place called Chard in Somerset. There were also stories from St Mark's, Gillingham, where David Watson was then a curate.

In 1968, Dr Martyn Lloyd-Jones was preaching through the early chapters of John's gospel and teaching his view on the baptism of the Holy Spirit, repeating and refining the material in his published sermons on Romans 8 and Ephesians 1. He was certainly not taking the then mainstream evangelical view of baptism in the Spirit when he said, 'We are so afraid of excesses, we are so afraid of being labelled in a certain way, that we claim the baptism of the Spirit to be something unconscious, non-experimental, a happening that does not affect a man's feelings. Such an argument is utterly unscriptural.'[1]

I heard a number of his sermons on the subject, so shortly before I left college, I wrote to Dr Lloyd-Jones stating I was a theological student (a rather grandiose term we used in those days). I explained that I was about to become a Baptist minister and asked him whether he could help me concerning the doctrine of the baptism in the Spirit. He replied by referring me to the work of R.A. Torrey, an evangelist, and a friend of D.L. Moody. He taught a very definite experience of baptism in the Holy Spirit, subsequent to conversion, as a vital empowering for Christian service. 'Every child of God is under the most solemn obligation to see to it that he definitely receives the Holy Spirit, not merely as a regenerating power and as an indwelling presence, but as a definite enduement with power, before he undertakes service of any kind for God.'[2]

I had come to believe that there was more than what had been my current spiritual experience up to then. I was nervous of getting into something weird, but reassured by the teachings of Dr Lloyd-Jones. I became the pastor of a small Baptist church in 1969. There were some 3000 Baptist Union churches in the country, and only a handful were growing. The baptismal figures for the churches were steadily dropping year by year and the term *church planting* was not one I had ever heard. There was desperate need for God to move in a new way.

As I entered the Baptist ministry, the charismatic bomb went off! It caused a real row in my own church and, generally, there was huge tension over it in many Baptist churches as well as in many other denominations.

The advance of the charismatic movement sharpened my own conviction that I needed to be baptised in the Holy Spirit. Like many others at that time, I was hungry and thirsty and seeking after God. Then, I had a very definite and distinct experience when I was baptised in the Spirit. Over the next few years this experience was to directly effect a thorough change in my theology about the church.

Rather more significantly, the reason that the New Churches exist today is largely rooted in the fact that years ago in traditional settings, individuals were baptised in the Holy Spirit and for many at that time those settings became too restrictive.

To be baptised in the Spirit was really the first domino down. Worship, spiritual gifts, elders and spiritual authority,

'Ephesians 4 ministries', and new churches: all these were to follow.

Today we are familiar with the existence of many charismatic churches, but is there a loss of the early emphasis on being baptised in the Holy Spirit? Is there a lack of the hungering and thirsting element that some of us knew years ago? Perhaps it can be assumed that since people come to the New Churches that they are baptised in the Holy Spirit? Or maybe there is less certainty about our theology on the subject. This is what I want to address in this chapter. Could it be true that years ago our theology may have been more raw but our experience more real?

In the early days of the charismatic movement, baptism in the Spirit was seen as distinct from conversion or at least a very distinct element within conversion. Today there are those who would either claim to be charismatic, or favourable to the charismatic, who are definitely teaching that baptism in the Spirit is automatically received at conversion. They say every Christian is baptised in the Holy Spirit, though later he or she can be *filled* with the Holy Spirit.

Terminology

Arguing over terms is foolish. What some of us might mean as being *baptised* in the Spirit is exactly what others may refer to as being *filled* with the Spirit. There is no difference either in experience or in effect. If that is the case then we would be silly to fall out over the terminology. But I believe that there may be more at stake here and if what we previously called 'Baptism in the Spirit' is now to be termed as 'Filling with the Spirit' it can, in practice, lead to a different expectation of the Spirit's working.

There is a fluid use of terms in the New Testament that can be frankly confusing. Several different expressions are used that refer to the same spiritual blessing. From Acts 1 to Acts 9 they include 'baptised with the Spirit', 'coming upon', 'receiving power', 'being filled', 'the promise of the Father'. All these expressions seem to point to the same spiritual experience. Interestingly, the same fluid, interchangeable use of terms occurs again when Cornelius and his family come to faith in Acts 10 and 11. We read: the Holy Spirit came on them all; the Holy Spirit is poured on them; they receive the Holy Spirit. Peter explains all this, when he gives an account of these events to the church in Jerusalem, as being a fulfilment of Jesus' own words: 'John baptised with water but you will be baptised with the Holy Spirit' (Acts 11:16). This, says Peter, is exactly what happened to them, just as it happened to us.

I believe that this fluid terminology for the work of the Holy Spirit should caution us against the idea that we can easily fit him into our systems or analyses: we cannot even fit him neatly into our terminology.

A key text

One of the key texts in this matter is 1 Corinthians 12:13, where we read, 'we were all baptised by one spirit into one body'. There can be no doubt that for those of us who want to thoroughly explain scripture on this subject, this verse holds a crucial place. For those supporting baptism in the Spirit as something distinct from conversion, the emphasis has tended to be that the Holy Spirit is the agent. He baptises and the church is what we are baptised into, so every Christian has been baptised by the Holy Spirit into the church, into the body of Christ. Therefore this verse has nothing to do with baptism in the Holy Spirit.

Years ago, John Stott challenged this with a legitimate alternative translation: that we are all baptised in (not by) the Holy Spirit into one body.[3] So he argues that every Christian is baptised in the Spirit. In practice, this means every Christian is automatically baptised in the Holy Spirit at conversion.

Charismatics, however, especially those of reformed persuasion, drew great heart from Dr Lloyd-Jones' vigorous championing of the former interpretation, more recently supported in print by Michael Eaton.[4] Dr Lloyd-Jones argued that this verse has absolutely nothing to do with baptism in the Spirit, but is only to do with what is true for every Christian: that we are automatically placed into the universal body of Christ and that this is the work of the Holy Spirit. Michael Eaton says that this is agreed by virtually everyone. An appeal to the majority verdict is always a risk, but he says it is agreed by virtually everyone that 1 Corinthians 12:13 speaks of a placement into the organism of the church, which is not necessarily experiential. In practice, however, many respected writers who are reckoned to be at least positive about the charismatic movement take issue with that interpretation, including J.I. Packer, Michael Green, Richard Lovelace in *Dynamics of Spiritual Renewal*, as well as John Wimber, Wayne Grudem and Gordon Fee.

We are dealing here with some finely detailed points of exegesis including the precise meaning of the little Greek word 'en'. Do we translate it as 'in' or 'by'? Also we need the right understanding of Greek cases used in particular constructions or with particular words. To give the flavour of this here, Gordon Fee says, 'Nowhere else does the dative form with *baptise* imply agency (that is, the Spirit does the baptising), but always refers to the element in which one is baptised.'[5]

In other words, he is making an appeal to the New Testament use of language and claims that the only possible way to understand 1 Corinthians 12:13 is as a reference to our all being baptised in the Holy Spirit with the purpose of enjoying a common life in the body of Christ. 'The purpose of our common experience of the Holy Spirit is that we are formed into one body. Hence we were all immersed in the one Spirit, so as to become one body.'[6] This inevitably means that all Christians are baptised in the Holy Spirit at conversion.

Wayne Grudem argues that if in six out of seven New Testament references 'baptised *in* the Spirit' is the correct translation, then it is only right that we translate it the same way in the seventh occurrence which is 1 Corinthians 12:13. He adds these important words: 'no matter how we translate it, it seems hard to deny that the original readers would have seen this phrase as referring to the same thing as the other six verses, because for them the words were the same.' It seems to me that is a pretty convincing and watertight argument.[7]

Wayne Grudem is writing a systematic theology. There is one great danger with systematic theology: it can be too systematic. The challenge is to try and get everything to fit into your system. When we are trying to understand the Trinity, the incarnation or the work of the Holy Spirit, I suggest that we are taking on something that is bigger than our systems!

Grudem appeals for a consistent understanding of the phrase 'Baptism in the Spirit'. He says that it seems appropriate to conclude that 1 Corinthians 12:13 refers to baptism in or with the Holy Spirit. This would mean that as far as the apostle Paul is concerned, baptism in the Holy Spirit occurred at conversion. All the Corinthians were baptised in the Holy Spirit and the result was that they became members of the body of Christ. Baptism in the Holy Spirit therefore must refer to the activity of the Holy Spirit at the beginning of the Christian life.

So both Fee and Grudem are concluding that baptism in the Holy Spirit is what happens to all Christians at conversion. And because Wayne Grudem is a systematic theologian every other scripture now has to be forced into that box.

At this point it is worth introducing David Pawson's view on this subject. Pawson is probably closer to what has been seen as the typical charismatic view of baptism in the Holy Spirit but he agrees with Fee and Grudem that the reference in 1 Corinthians 12:13 is to baptism *in* the Holy Spirit and not to baptism *by* the Holy Spirit into the body of Christ.

Pawson believes in a *distinct experience* of baptism in the Holy Spirit, so how can he equate the view of all being baptised in one Spirit with the fact that there are many Christians who appear to lack the experience? Pawson's answer seems to be that in the New Testament period, all Christians had enjoyed that experience, all were baptised in the Holy Spirit, and to suggest anything else would have astonished Paul and the Corinthian Christians.[8] The deduction from Pawson's argument is that today, because of poor teaching or non-expectation, there are Christians who have not been baptised in the Holy Spirit, and this is abnormal. It is not normal Christianity but it does not exclude believers from the body of Christ.

The accounts in Acts

The accounts of incidents in the book of Acts have always been a fruitful area for debates over charismatic issues. What no-one can deny and, as far as I am aware, does not even try to deny is that the disciples were baptised in the Holy Spirit on the day of Pentecost even though before nine o'clock that morning they were already Christians.

Fixing the time of the disciples' conversion is a challenge. For example, what about Peter at Caesarea Philippi saying, 'You are the Christ, the Son of the living God' (Matthew 16:16). Was he regenerate at that time? My own view is that by the time of the so-called insufflation of John 20 (when Jesus breathes on the disciples), the disciples compare as closely as possible to us in terms of conversion. So we read that the risen Christ comes to them, breathes on them, and he says to them 'Receive the Holy Spirit' (John 20:22). At this point the disciples are clearly believers in the risen Christ, and Jesus has breathed on them the life-giving breath of God: the 'ruach' of God is in them.

I believe there is even then some real influence of the Holy Spirit at work in them, a point we will pick up later. Whatever we may want to say about *when* the disciples were born again as Christians, I would suggest that they certainly were by John chapter 20. All the commentators I can find agree on this point. This includes Fee and Grudem and therefore they also have to agree that the coming of the Holy Spirit on the disciples at Pentecost is subsequent to their conversion.

Those who take Grudem's position on baptism in the Holy Spirit will argue the uniqueness of this situation: Pentecost marks the beginning of the dispensation of the Holy Spirit, therefore the disciples could not be baptised in the Holy Spirit until then. It was unique, but there was a separation between the two – conversion and later baptism in the Spirit – on that occasion.

Could that happen again? Yes, we find that Grudem accepts that it does happen again! This brings us to Acts 8:14–17 where we read about the Samaritans who were converted to Christ, and then the apostles came from Jerusalem and prayed with them to receive the Spirit. Why then was there an interval between conversion and the coming of the Holy Spirit? The argument is that with the ancient hostility between the Jews and the Samaritans, it was vital to avoid a split in the Christian era between Jewish and Samaritan churches, so the Holy Spirit was not manifested upon the Samaritan converts until representatives came from Jerusalem. They expressed solidarity with them as they prayed and laid hands on them, and then the Samaritans were baptised in the Holy Spirit.

Let us be clear: if those who hold the traditional charismatic view are made to feel vulnerable by the above interpretation of 1 Corinthians 12:13, which suggests that the reference is to baptism in the Spirit, not baptism by the Spirit, then Acts 8 is a point of real vulnerability for those wishing to teach that Spirit baptism is always automatic at conversion.

There is a real problem with the idea that representatives had to come from Jerusalem to show solidarity with converted Samaritans. It really does sound like trying to find an artificial reason to explain what doesn't fit a particular theological position. Surely, if it was essential to show solidarity between Jews and Samaritans, the vital issue is that the Samaritans should receive the Holy Spirit in exactly the same kind of way as the Jews. But it is only when the apostles laid hands on them that the Samaritans were baptised in the Holy Spirit and something very definite and distinct happened. We don't know what happened, it may well have been speaking in tongues, but to claim that dogmatically is an argument from silence or, indeed, prejudice. Certainly what did happen was convincing enough for Simon Magus to offer payment for the ability to help others receive the Holy Spirit. After all, he had been a magician, he knew about power.

Now if the Samaritans had received their baptism in the Holy Spirit at conversion, it would have been clear, distinct, obvious and experiential; clear enough to demonstrate that in fact they were receiving in just the same kind of way as the Jewish converts had received in Jerusalem. But Grudem and others want to argue that baptism in the Spirit is what happens to all at conversion, but it did not happen like that with the Samaritans. It happened later, so they have to find an exceptional reason to explain it.

I find their explanation unconvincing. Surely, what the apostles did by coming to Samaria was not to express solidarity but simply to set things right. The Samaritans had not received the Holy Spirit. The apostles were fulfilling their ministry and setting things right. I would also argue that if the Samaritans are exceptional, why couldn't we have other exceptions?

My real concern is this: if you insist that everyone is baptised in the Holy Spirit at conversion, you end up with a position that for many it is unconscious and not experiential.

A further point emerges with the conversion of Cornelius and friends in Acts 10: they are baptised in the Holy Spirit as they listen to the gospel. That is plain and explicit and it would therefore seem to support the view of Grudem and others who hold the same kind of view but it actually raises some other interesting issues.

We now find that we have a complex pattern emerging. The day of Pentecost is unique; the Samaritan Pentecost is delayed and needs special pleading from Grudem and others. Now we have a Gentile Pentecost with Cornelius being baptised in the Holy Spirit and this seems to fit; it takes place at the right time at the time of his conversion. But I would suggest that once we have got something of a complex pattern it could indicate that we might always have something of a complex pattern. Cornelius and company are not quite decent and in order anyway: they are baptised in the Holy Spirit before they are baptised in water. In fact, they are very probably baptised in the Holy Spirit before they have even said, 'Jesus Christ is Lord'.

It is very untidy, but the Holy Spirit is not as tidy as our systematic theology. He works sovereignly in his way. We cannot tell where he is coming from or where he is going. He doesn't do it by the textbook.

Acts 19 produces another interesting set of circumstances. Paul goes to Ephesus and finds a group of about twelve disciples. Were this group of twelve men Christians or not? The word disciple is used of them and Michael Eaton says 'definitely Christians' because that is the only way the word disciple is used in the New Testament. 'Definitely not Christians', says Wayne Grudem, 'but were converted when Paul preached to them'. Grudem, of course, has to say that, or he would have yet another exception to his position here with those already Christians being later baptised in the Holy Spirit, and he really cannot afford another exception. 'Immature Christians', says David Pawson.

In some ways we do not need to be too concerned as to whether or not they were Christians at this point. It is Paul's question that is the more fascinating part of this story. Acts chapter 19:2 has its own exegetical problems to do with the rules of Greek grammar. Should we read, *when* you believed or is it *after* you believed? Paul is asking whether they received the Spirit *when* they believed or *after* they believed. Either is possible, so let us take both.

We can understand the question as: Was there a time, either when or after you believed, that you received the Holy Spirit? Two enormously important conclusions result from that question. Evidently, you can believe and not receive. If that is not true, why did Paul ask the question?

Secondly, Paul means receiving the Holy Spirit *experientially*.

If that is not true, again, there is no point in asking the question. If they are baptised automatically in the Holy Spirit at conversion, then the question is simply 'Did you *believe*?' not 'Did you *receive*?' because if they believed, they would automatically have received. Paul's question can only have any meaning and relevance if there is something experiential in the baptism of the Holy Spirit.

After Paul had preached Christ and baptised these disciples in water, had they then been asked, 'Did you receive?' they could have said, 'Did we receive? We came out of the water, hands were laid on us and we spoke in tongues and prophesied. Did we receive? We certainly did.'

Summary

Firstly, there is a fluidity of terms used of the Holy Spirit that makes it difficult for anyone to be totally systematic in their terminology. The Holy Spirit is bigger than our words.

Secondly, 1 Corinthians 12:13 is clearly a key verse. While I would want to accept Lloyd-Jones' and Michael Eaton's exegesis that we are all baptised by one Spirit into one body, I have to confess that there are some weighty arguments from Grudem and Fee, who interpret that verse as meaning that all are baptised in one Spirit. However, Pawson's view must not be overlooked here. It is not simply a compromise; he is claiming that this verse reflects the *normal* situation. All Christians in the church of Corinth were baptised in the Holy Spirit. We are in the abnormal situation, where there are Christians who are not baptised in the Holy Spirit.

Thirdly, some were baptised in the Holy Spirit after conversion: the disciples on the day of Pentecost; the Samaritans; and maybe the twelve Ephesians. I have not even argued the same is surely true of the apostle Paul, and what do we make of the coming of the Holy Spirit on Jesus at the time of his baptism by John?

Michael Green says that we must not build a doctrine on

the experience of the apostle Paul. Of course Green says that: Paul's experience doesn't fit *his* doctrine! Similarly, you can argue, Jesus' situation was unique, but how many unique non-typical events can you claim simply because they do not fit your theology? If every occasion described in the New Testament is abnormal, what is normal? Cornelius is baptised in the Holy Spirit at conversion before being baptised in water: also gloriously untidy!

Fourthly, if every Christian today is baptised in the Holy Spirit at conversion, then clearly it can be non-experiential: 'All Christians are but they don't know it'. To encourage later fillings of the Holy Spirit which are experiential may be desirable, even biblical, but here we can lose ground in this matter. After all, if we are all baptised in the Holy Spirit, in a sense we really have already got it all. Hence Dr Lloyd-Jones' famous question in this regard, 'Got it all? Got it at your conversion? Well, where is it, I ask?'

Fifthly, it is undeniable that in the New Testament, baptism in the Holy Spirit *is* always experiential. It is true of the disciples; it is true of the Samaritans; it is true of Cornelius and his family; of the twelve Ephesians, let alone Jesus and Paul. We have not yet looked at the exact nature of the experience, but in the New Testament they knew they had received and so did those who witnessed it. William Barclay observes that no one received the Holy Spirit unconsciously in the New Testament.

So, the terminology is fluid, but there is a real case for arguing that baptism in the Holy Spirit is not automatic at conversion. Even at the level of metaphor, 'baptism' is a good word to describe the first conscious overwhelming of the Holy Spirit. What I believe is clear and must not be minimised, is that baptism in the Spirit is always a definite conscious experience. I suggest the term 'baptised in the Holy Spirit' is the one best retained for a Christian's first conscious experiential encounter with the Holy Spirit, whether that takes place at conversion or later. It is an experience of God.

What is 'baptism in the Spirit'?

We can become weak in our doctrine of baptism in the Spirit unless we are clear on what we mean. If we take a traditional Pentecostal view, that when a person is baptised in the Spirit the initial evidence is always speaking in tongues, it is easy for the idea to arise that baptism in the Spirit *is* speaking in tongues. That can create a situation where the pressure is on to force a person to speak in tongues. On the other hand, if we do not insist on tongues as the initial evidence (which must surely be correct from an overview of the New Testament), then we can get what I call the 'warm feeling syndrome'. As long as the person claims *something* or 'I've got a nice tingly feeling', we settle for that.

In a cartoon a lady is speaking to her pastor. She says: 'I'm not sure I'm dead to sin but I did feel a bit faint once'. She might get away with saying, 'I'm not sure I was baptised in the Holy Spirit, but I did have a nice warm feeling once.' Push that even further and we can be in danger of thinking that simply because we prayed for someone to be baptised in the Holy Spirit it must have happened, which is very close to the 'take it by faith' idea, 'You've asked, therefore it's happened. Don't worry about the evidence.'

There are two approaches I want to make to understand the nature of baptism in the Spirit. The first is:

A power encounter

In Acts 1:4–8, the promise of Jesus to the disciples is that they would receive the gift of the Holy Spirit and would then be witnesses in Jerusalem and Judea, Samaria and to the ends of the earth. There is a promise of power with the promise of the baptism in the Holy Spirit. There will be an encounter with the power of God because of an encounter with God himself in the person of the Holy Spirit. The result of this will be a witnessing community, which is exactly what happened, of course, on the day of Pentecost.

The first time I saw somebody sovereignly baptised in the Holy Spirit was in 1970, when I took a small group from the church that I was leading to Barney Coombes' Basingstoke Baptist Church (as it was then).

In the group was a young wife who had recently come to our church, and was incredibly shy. She was undoubtedly a Christian, but completely unable to articulate or speak of her faith at all and not even prepared to be baptised in water because she was so timid and nervous. In Basingstoke the Holy Spirit fell upon her with such power that she was literally knocked off her feet. Although she did not speak in tongues until several weeks later, within a fortnight she was baptised in water and speaking out her testimony to everybody, in the church and outside. She had an encounter with God the Holy Spirit that empowered her to witness in that way.

The second approach to understanding the nature of the baptism of the Holy Spirit is through:

The sealing work of the Spirit

We need to pick up on the term 'seal' in connection with baptism in the Holy Spirit. John 7:37–39 tells us that up to that point in Jesus' ministry the Holy Spirit had not been given since Jesus had not yet been glorified. So there is a promise inferred that the Holy Spirit would be given when Jesus was glorified. Jesus promises baptism in the Holy Spirit (Acts 1:5), and Peter talking of the Spirit on the day of Pentecost says, 'The promise is for you and your children' (Acts 2:39), so the Holy Spirit is again and again the *promised* Holy Spirit.

Later there comes a fulfilment of the promise in the lives of those who are redeemed, when they receive the Spirit (e.g. Galatians 3:14.). Moreover, the promise fulfilled involves *being marked with a seal*. 'Having believed, you were marked in him with a seal, the promised Holy Spirit' (Ephesians 1:13). The promised Holy Spirit marks us with a seal, so 2 Corinthians 1:21,22 says, 'He anointed us, *set his seal of ownership on us*, and put his Spirit in our hearts as a deposit, guaranteeing what is to come'.

The seal is to be understood as a mark of ownership – we have been sealed, branded – we belong to God. The sealing work of the Spirit is a deposit, or first instalment guaranteeing what is to come. There is something imparted to us when the promise of the coming of the Spirit is fulfilled and when we are sealed that guarantees our future. We have a taster; although the best is yet to come!

The experiential nature of this sealing is indicated when we read: 'God sent the spirit of his Son into our hearts, the Spirit who calls out "*Abba*, Father"'(Galatians 4:6). In Romans 8 we read that we receive the spirit of sonship, and by him we cry '*Abba*, Father'. If we are children, then we are heirs that we might also share in his glory, and the Holy Spirit bears witness with our spirit (Romans 8:15–17). The authenticity of our belonging to God is sealed by the Spirit and causes us to cry '*Abba*, Father'. We are the heirs of God and will share the glory of Christ in that inheritance.

So there is a clear and definite link between all these verses on the Holy Spirit. We have a clear line of doctrine. When the promise is fulfilled (best termed 'the baptism in the Holy Spirit'), then that event must be experiential. It will be like 'streams of living water' that flow from within us: that's what Jesus said in John 7 as he promised the Spirit. There was a first fulfilment of that promise on the day of Pentecost, which was clearly very experiential. For us to cry out '*Abba*, Father' is again, surely, experiential, and for the Spirit to witness with our spirit that we are truly the sons and heirs of God, with a glorious inheritance in store, is what produces a surge of excitement within us.

The sealing is a result of our being baptised in the Holy Spirit, and because of this we freely cry out concerning God's fatherhood. We have a deposit, a first instalment, giving us the guarantee that the best is yet to be! Therefore, when we are baptised in the Holy Spirit we encounter the power of God but we also get something by way of an inward assurance of God's love for us, which we then begin to express outwardly. It may be in tongues, it may be in prophecy, it may be in witness, or it may be in praise. But there is an outward verbal overflow of an inward assurance.

I am not saying that every person baptised in the Holy Spirit will say: 'I have now received an inward assurance and I can so feel the Holy Spirit witnessing with my spirit that I now wish to cry out "*Abba*, Father"'. It is rather more spontaneous than that. Nevertheless, I do believe that something outward has to result from the fact that we have experienced God in the Holy Spirit.

When?

This is a most absorbing question. The normal Christian life would seem to be a life in which baptism in the Holy Spirit quickly follows repentance and faith. In fact, a normal Christian conversion, we could argue, should include baptism in the Holy Spirit as part of the process but a distinct part of it. What, then do we say about those who are baptised in the Holy Spirit some time after their conversion? What was their relationship to the Spirit before that happened? If for some or many there is a gap between conversion and baptism in the Holy Spirit, where is the Holy Spirit between those events? This is something of a theological nightmare and it has both a doctrinal and a practical aspect.

In the story of the insufflation in John 20:19–23, a huge debate rages around verses 21,22, where Jesus comes to his disciples, commissions them, breathes on them and says, 'Peace be with you. Receive the Holy Spirit.' Now, did the disciples at that time of insufflation receive the Holy Spirit in some way, or not?

Calvin says they did, and so does Martyn Lloyd-Jones. D.A. Carson's conclusion, after much detailed exegesis and rejection of other alternatives is that they did not in any sense receive the Holy Spirit at this time. He suggests this is an acted parable (his expression), pointing to Pentecost. The expression sounds impressive, but it is unconvincing. He says: 'There is no intrinsic reason for thinking that the imperative "Receive the Holy Spirit" must be experienced immediately'.[9] I suggest one intrinsic reason: that's what it says!

Leon Morris proposes that it is the teaching of the New Testament that there are diversities of gifts but the same Spirit and this issue is probably to be solved along these lines. 'It is false alike to the New Testament and to Christian experience to maintain that there is but one gift of the Holy Spirit; rather, the Holy Spirit is continually manifesting Himself in new ways, so John tells of one gift, and Luke of another.'[10]

This means that we can take the Scripture as it reads. It saves us from denying the activity of the Holy Spirit in the lives of the disciples before Pentecost, but it still leaves us with an authentic baptism of the Holy Spirit at Pentecost. By implication, for Christians today with a gap between their conversion and baptism in the Holy Spirit, it allows us to affirm the genuine activity of the Holy Spirit in believers' lives in the interim.

In practical terms, those not yet baptised in the Holy Spirit should ask and seek God for it with hunger, thirst, seriousness and faith, just as many of us did in the early years of the charismatic movement, even though some of us had already been Christians for years by that time.

Michael Eaton says this: 'I ... believe that subsequent to Christian conversion, one's experience may catch up with what one possesses objectively and in principle from conversion onwards. The term 'Baptism with the Holy Spirit' ought in my judgement to be used not of what is in principle given at Christian initiation (conversion) but of what is in experience known, which may or may not take place at the time of coming to Christ'.[11]

Being practical

We need to say something on the practical side. In his teaching on this subject I venture to suggest that Dr Lloyd-Jones is in one way very unhelpful. He is wonderfully helpful in urging the Christian to seek what he has not yet experienced, to be baptised in the Spirit. But he is unhelpful in that the only examples he ever seems to give are of highly dramatic experiences of the very greatest preachers.

He was very fond of telling the story of D.L. Moody walking down the streets in New York, praying to be baptised in the Holy Spirit and so overwhelmed by the Holy Spirit that he asked the Lord to stay his hand lest he should die. He then preached the same sermons he had already been preaching and, whereas before only a few people had been converted, now dozens or hundreds were being converted by these same messages after he had been baptised in the Holy Spirit. It's a wonderful story, but not everyone's experience is going to be as intense as that, and if we only use this kind of story it can appear to put the experience out of reach.

Also, those baptised in the Holy Spirit can most certainly be subsequently and sovereignly filled with the Holy Spirit. This will be true for a particular occasion and at a particular time. There are examples of that, of course, in the New Testament. In Acts 4:31 we read of the disciples, already baptised in the Holy Spirit on the day of Pentecost, gathering together for a prayer meeting when they are filled with the Holy Spirit and also filled with boldness to preach the word of God. Again, Peter (baptised in the Holy Spirit on the day of Pentecost) gets up before the Jewish authorities and is filled with the Holy Spirit and able to speak boldly (Acts 4:8).

To put it in the simplest terms that I can state, I believe the New Testament position is this. When a person comes to faith in Christ they should seek to be baptised in the Holy Spirit, for the promise is for them. This baptism will be experiential in nature and as the person encounters the power of

God there will be an inner witness of the Spirit that will result in some outward manifestation; most commonly, but not definitely, speaking in tongues. Subsequent to this there can be numerous other times when a believer is filled with the Spirit which will in some measure reproduce or reflect the initial baptism in the Spirit.

For those Christians who, for whatever reason, have not been baptised in the Spirit there should be the teaching and encouragement for them to seek the fulfilment of the promise in their own lives.

Therefore the question still remains relevant: 'Did you receive the Holy Spirit when you believed?' (Acts 19:2).

Notes

1. *God's Ultimate Purpose*, D.M. Lloyd-Jones, The Banner of Truth Trust, 1978, p. 269.
2. *The Person and Work of the Holy Spirit*, R.A. Torrey, Zondervan, 1973, p. 200.
3. *Baptism and Fullness: The work of the Holy Spirit today*, J.R.W. Stott, IVP, 1975.
4. *Baptism with the Spirit in the teaching of Martyn Lloyd-Jones*, Michael A. Eaton, IVP, 1989.
5. *God's Empowering Presence*, Gordon D. Fee, Hendrickson Publishers, Inc., 1994, p. 181.
6. As above, p. 182.
7. Wayne Grudem's teaching on baptism in the Spirit can be found on pages 764–784 of *Systematic Theology*, Wayne Grudem, IVP, 1994.
8. *Jesus Baptises In One Holy Spirit*, David Pawson, Hodder and Stoughton, 1997.
9. *The Gospel according to John*, D.A. Carson, IVP, 1991, pp. 649–653.
10. *The Gospel according to John*, Leon Morris. Marshall, Morgan and Scott, 1971, p. 847.
11. *Baptism with the Spirit in the teaching of Martyn Lloyd-Jones*, Michael A. Eaton, IVP, 1989, p. 233.

Chapter 10   # Worship
            The overflow of our hearts

As a young person I belonged to what would now be spoken of as a traditional Baptist church. I was leading a Baptist church when the first waves of charismatic renewal began to roll in. Along with people claiming that they had been baptised in the Spirit there was also a demand for our worship to change. My guess is that if people had only testified to baptism in the Spirit and simply left it there then other Christians would have even been encouraging of those who were speaking of a new experience of God. But to attempt a change from a fairly fixed pattern of worship was what really began to disturb other believers.

Even in the 1960s there was already discussion of the form of worship in Baptist churches. Some were suggesting the value of a more liturgical approach. When invited to preach at another Baptist church an order of service would often be sent, with a note that the visiting preacher (who in those days led all the worship as well) was to feel perfectly free to vary the order. In truth, however, about the only possible alternatives were to swap around the place of a prayer and the Bible reading. Even to have sung two hymns, one after another without a break, would somehow have seemed rather shocking, even bizarre.

Charismatic renewal really challenged these fixed forms of worship. Suddenly there were new songs and hymns and individuals began to raise their hands and to clap. Looking back now there were some extraordinary reactions. People who were bold enough to raise their hands in worship often felt they were doing something incredibly daring and those observing were sometimes incredibly offended. I listened to a Baptist pastor complaining that he had sat in a meeting where the person in front of him had raised his hands and actually blocked his view of the front of the building!

Early in the 1970s I attended an annual reunion at my old training college and a very well known Keswick Convention speaker had been asked to address us on the subject of worship. There was something approaching feverish excitement ahead of his message, as so many Baptist churches were now either 'going charismatic' or strongly opposing going charismatic or experimenting with some new approaches to worship. The brother spoke for an hour on the subject of preaching without a single mention of worship.

In a way it summed up the views of many at that time, that worship was just a preliminary run in to the real thing, which is the preaching. I am one of those who continue to believe that preaching must hold a central place within the life of a worshipping community and that to restore the church to a true biblical expression of church life we must, like the early Christians, be devoted to the apostles' teachings. However, worship has its own vital and central place amongst the community of God's people. That was true in the Old Testament and in the New Testament, and will be true in heaven forever.

These days there is a tendency to analyse times of worship and we can often now discuss the merit of particular worship leaders. What we must not lose sight of here is that worship is for God. Once we start analysing, we are in danger of bringing our criticisms and judgements according to whether we have enjoyed the worship. We should perhaps be rather more concerned with whether God has enjoyed the worship!

When God was giving the Ten Commandments to Moses he spoke of the fact that he is a jealous God and that worship is not to be given to any other god. This seems to suggest that God is self-centred and as believers we would tend to warn people against being jealous and self-centred. But we need to appreciate God is God. There is no one more supreme; there is no one more exalted than God. God is the highest good in the universe. Nothing and no one can surpass him now or forever. Therefore, God must be right to call all worship to himself and allow no space for the worship of others who will always be totally inferior. We need to see God as God and always worthy of all our worship.

> For great is the Lord and most worthy of praise;
> he is to be feared above all gods.
> For all the gods of the nations are idols,
> but the Lord made the heavens.
> (Psalm 96:4, 5)

When we worship God, we should understand that this is really an overflow of what is inside us. It is right to appreciate that worship is essentially a whole life, committed to God. Paul says, 'Therefore, I urge you, brothers, in view of God's mercy, to offer your bodies as living sacrifices, holy and pleasing to God – this is your spiritual act of worship' (Romans 12:1). So worship is not something that we confine to an hour on a Sunday morning, but it is a whole life lived for God. And as our life is contained in a physical body, it is with our physical body that we live our life for God.

Having said that, the Bible makes it very clear that there are times of praise when, from the heart, but also through our lips we worship the Lord. When we worship God in this way we should not be waiting for God to do something, like making us feel better or making us feel particularly happy. We praise God because he has already done something. He has saved us, put his Spirit within us, made us his children and promised us glory.

There should be more than enough already in us to overflow with praise. I like to think of worship as an explosion of joy. 'Though you have not seen him, you love him; and even though you do not see him now, you believe in him and are filled with an inexpressible and glorious joy, for you are

receiving the goal of your faith, the salvation of your souls'
(1 Peter 1:8, 9). Inexpressible joy here actually means joy that
is so great it cannot be expressed to the full, not that we do not
even try!

Peter was writing to a church facing persecution and to a
people who had never seen Christ in the flesh. But they had a
deep inner conviction about their salvation, they loved Christ
and they were filled with joy. This conviction, love and joy evidently exploded into passionate praise. The reality of what God
has done for us, as well as who God is, should always be more
than enough to cause us to be overflowing with worship.

It is true that sometimes we need to stir ourselves to worship. The circumstances of life, our feelings and emotions, can
on some days, be at a level where we need more than loud
music and a strong beat to cause us to overflow. There are
times that we need to speak to ourselves, which in a Christian
is the first sign of common sense and not the first sign of madness.

> Praise the Lord, O my soul,
> and forget not all his benefits –
> who forgives all your sins
> and heals all your diseases,
> who redeems your life from the pit
> and crowns you with love and compassion (Psalm 103:2–4).

We may need to speak to ourselves like this. To recall all our
benefits so that we may again 'Praise the Lord'. At other times
other believers can encourage our worship. 'Speak to one
another with psalms, hymns and spiritual songs' (Ephesians
5:19). In a time of praise and worship, although our focus is on
God, there is also a sense in which we are speaking to one
another, or instructing one another. A prayer adoring God for
what he has done, a reading with words that exalt the greatness of God, can be the way that other believers speak to us and
instruct us so that our own praise begins to overflow.

From the Bible there are three important elements that will help us to see worship and praise restored to the church in a way that more fully declares that God is worthy.

Celebration

The Old Testament is full of worship and the worship has about it a glorious spirit of celebration. Again and again the particular focus of this celebration is the greatness of God himself, often seen in creation, but also the saving work of God for the nation as witnessed in the deliverance from slavery in Egypt. So we read:

> Great is the Lord and most worthy of praise;
> his greatness no one can fathom.
> One generation will commend your works to another;
> they will tell of your mighty acts.
> They will speak of the glorious splendour of your majesty,
> and I will meditate on your wonderful works (Psalm 145:3-5).

And here is Moses singing of deliverance from Egypt and safe passage across the Red Sea:

> Who among the gods is like you, O Lord?
> Who is like you –
> majestic in holiness,
> awesome in glory,
> working wonders? (Exodus 15:11).

The note of celebration is then heightened as we read on:

> Then Miriam the prophetess, Aaron's sister, took a tambourine in
> her hand and all the women followed her, with tambourines and
> dancing. Miriam sang to them:
> 'Sing to the Lord,
> for he is highly exalted.

> *The horse and its rider*
> *he has hurled into the sea' (Exodus 15:20,21).*

The sense of celebration is particularly strong in the very last Psalm:

> *Praise him with the sounding of the trumpet,*
> *praise him with the harp and lyre,*
> *praise him with tambourine and dancing,*
> *praise him with the strings and flute,*
> *praise him with the clash of cymbals,*
> *praise him with resounding cymbals (Psalm 150:3–5).*

It is evident just from these few scriptures that worship could be loud, that many musical instruments were used and it was physical. Worshippers clapped their hands and danced. Worship and praise were times of great celebration.

God is as mighty today as he was in the time of the Old Testament. Therefore we have reason to celebrate today.

God has done more for us in delivering us from slavery to sin and condemnation through the work of Christ than he ever did for the nation of Israel. Israel crossed a sea. We have crossed from death to life because of the mighty works of God. There is reason for our celebration.

We do not go into a church meeting to be quiet because that is reverent. When we are the church, we are a people called out to praise our God. Worship will at times be noisy; it will involve a wide range of musical instruments. How can we even keep still? Let's raise our hands, clap and dance. Let us celebrate what our great God has done for us. Arguably this *is* reverent; we are genuinely revering God, as we celebrate his greatness and wonderful works of salvation. There are also times of God-filled silence and stillness, which often come after a time of noisy celebration, when the presence of God seems overwhelming and no one feels inclined to move or make a sound. But to deliberately adopt an attitude that true worship must always be expressed in quietness and stillness can actually seem inappropriate and irreverent in the light of God's saving action for us.

Participation

In the New Testament we see an encouragement for the different members of the body of Christ to participate in the worship. This is important for we are not just meant to attend times of worship, but to participate in and contribute to the praise and worship of God's people.

> *What then shall we say, brothers? When you come together, everyone has a hymn, or a word of instruction, a revelation, a tongue or an interpretation. All of these must be done for the strengthening of the church (1 Corinthians 14:26).*

I find it interesting that Paul says, 'everyone has a hymn' etc. rather than 'someone has a hymn.' The reality is that if everyone in a congregation of 500, 100 or even 50 were to bring a contribution then our meetings would be intolerably long. Surely the emphasis here is that everyone will come with the willingness to contribute, but in the actual meeting, some will.

To come with a desire to contribute is a positive attitude towards worshipping with other believers. Paul is obviously making it clear that there are different ways of contributing without exhausting the possibilities. But every contribution is to be done for building up the body of Christ. Paradoxically, this means that sometimes we won't contribute. We may feel stirred with a prophetic word, but to bring it during this particular meeting could unhelpfully change the whole direction of the meeting and therefore not strengthen the church. We should be willing to bring a contribution, but also sensitive so that sometimes we hold back from doing so, for the good of the whole church.

I love the risk of worship where participation is genuinely

expected. There is the chance of nothing really happening but there is also the possibility of glory. Fortunately, in my experience there has been a lot more glory than nothingness when prayers, prophecy, songs and preaching all complement one another and times of worship can seem like a touch of heaven on earth. There are some meetings when the contributions can seem dull and uninspired but it is worth persevering for the times of glory.

Revelation

Here I am talking about the Book of Revelation. Key elements to worship are celebration, participation and revelation. But by revelation I mean that our worship should reflect something of the worship we read of in that book. In Revelation there are numerous occasions when we are given a glimpse of the church worshipping in heaven. The church in heaven is not unrelated to the church on the earth, it is simply promoted! There ought to be something about the church presently on the earth that is at least some reflection, even if only a pale reflection, of the church in the age to come.

This also applies in our worship. Indeed the Book of Revelation, which is essentially about the victory of God, often helps us in our worship services when readings from chapters 4 and 5 have certainly stirred the congregation in its own time of praise.

> *Whenever the living creatures give glory, honour and thanks to him who sits on the throne and who lives for ever and ever, the twenty-four elders fall down before him who sits on the throne, and worship him who lives for ever and ever. They lay their crowns before the throne and say: 'You are worthy, our Lord and God, to receive glory and honour and power, for you created all things, and by your will they were created and have their being'* (Revelation 4:9–11).

Again we read,

> *Worthy is the Lamb, who was slain, to receive power and wealth*
> *and wisdom and strength and honour and glory and praise!*
> *(Revelation 5:12).*

Readings like this give us a glimpse into the worship of heaven and certainly draw out our worship on the earth.

In Revelation 7 we read of those who have been redeemed from every nation, tribe, people and language and who stand together before the throne, where they adore the Lamb and in a loud voice cry out:

> *Salvation belongs to our God.*
> *who sits on the throne,*
> *and to the Lamb (Revelation 7:10).*

Here we see that all the redeemed people of God are together in worship. The church has not always had a good record of believers worshipping together. In the days of apartheid in South Africa there was an absolute determination in many churches that black and white peoples should worship apart. In heaven, all the peoples will come together as one people, sharing and celebrating a common redemption, as they worship before the throne. Such a picture should stir us now to demonstrate that we are one people and one nation, called out of all the peoples and all the nations to declare the praise of God together.

Near the end of the Book of Revelation there are some very noisy celebrations:

> *Then I heard what sounded like a great multitude, like the roar*
> *of rushing waters and like loud peals of thunder, shouting:*
> *'Hallelujah!*
> *For our Lord God Almighty reigns.*
> *Let us rejoice and be glad*

and give him glory!
For the wedding of the Lamb has come,
and his bride has made herself ready.
Fine linen, bright and clean, was given her to wear'
(Revelation 19:6–8).

Once again there is a call to worship and celebration as the church and Christ – the bride and the bridegroom – come together for a marriage that means they will genuinely live happily ever after.

To catch something of the spirit of the Book of Revelation in our worship means that we do indeed celebrate the victory of God.

Men and women praise footballers and scream and shout at pop idols. Men talk of great goals that have been scored in matches and women (and many men) will spend time admiring fashion and jewellery. Men (and many women) will look adoringly at some splendid model of a car. There is a lot of attention and even worship given to that which is transient and often trivial.

A great God sits on the throne of heaven. He is the Sovereign Lord over all creation and all history. This God is working wonders, as even today, because of the Son he has sent, the blood of the Lamb will redeem many thousands around the world. Today there will be more worshippers of Jesus who will sing their praises on the earth and will join a chorus of praise that will never, ever cease.

The church today is being restored to be a worshipping community with celebration, participation and even reflecting something of the joy of heaven that we read of in the Book of Revelation.

Chapter 11   Gifts
               To bless the church

The new charismatic churches strongly believe that all the spiritual gifts mentioned in the New Testament are for the church throughout history and therefore for today. More and more this seems to have been generally accepted by the evangelical churches as a whole today and comparatively few now contest this on biblical grounds.

One scripture that has sometimes been used to suggest that spiritual gifts died out after the New Testament era has been from 1 Corinthians 13. 'For we know in part and we prophesy in part, but when perfection comes, the imperfect disappears' (vv. 9,10). So while acknowledging that words of knowledge and prophesy exist as spiritual gifts (and by implication other gifts as well) there is a teaching here that one day these gifts will disappear. The question is when? The answer given in 1 Corinthians 13 is when the 'perfect' comes. But what is the 'perfect'? Some have suggested that it is the scripture itself. So now that we have the full canon of scripture, and indeed have had it for many centuries, then it can be assumed that spiritual gifts have long since ceased.

But in fact this is the one thing that these verses of scripture cannot mean. When Paul wrote to Corinth the church would not have understood 'perfect' as referring to the New Testament canon of scripture, because they would have had no concept that such a canon would be formed. Indeed not even Paul knew that when he wrote 1 Corinthians 13. It is impossible therefore for the 'perfect' to refer to the scripture because for both Paul and the Corinthian church the idea would have been meaningless at that time.

The Greek word for 'perfection' (*teleion*) has the sense of consummation and would therefore be pointing to the end of history and the return of Christ. When that happens then the need for spiritual gifts will cease completely.

There is something else to be noted here by those who have suggested that all spiritual gifts have ceased. There has to be some 'explanation' of the 'gifts' that do operate in the church today. The obvious conclusion therefore by those who deny the gifts is that they are counterfeit gifts. The most extreme position is to say that they are demonic. Indeed, some have suggested this, especially with regard to speaking in tongues, seeing this as the deception of demons.

This is a highly dangerous suggestion. In the New Testament, the gifts that we read of are given by the Holy Spirit (1 Corinthians 12:7–11). If speaking in tongues is a genuine gift of the Holy Spirit, but then denounced as a demonic activity, this could be seen as what Jesus warned of as blasphemy against the Holy Spirit (Matthew 12:31).

However, I do not believe that this is actually blasphemy against the Holy Spirit. Such sin is totally deliberate and could only be committed by those who hate God. Those who denounce tongues as being of the devil actually love God and want to defend his name and his glory. But they are in danger of being very wrong by the testimony of scripture itself.

Seeking the Gifts

Charismatic Christians certainly do not always get everything right in the matter of spiritual gifts and a typical example of a misunderstanding arises out of 1 Corinthians 14:1: 'Follow the way of love and eagerly desire spiritual gifts, especially the gift of prophecy'. This verse, wrongly understood, has launched a thousand anxieties. It raises the question, what is my gift? Many Christians will say they eagerly desire spiritual gifts, but what is their particular gift? And if they are not sure they know, then they can become very concerned.

This is an unnecessary anxiety. What is not obvious in the English translation of this verse is that in the original Greek text it is cast in the plural. So Paul is not essentially instructing an individual to seek spiritual gifts, a common way of reading it, but he is instructing the whole church at Corinth to eagerly desire the gifts. The concern therefore, should not be, 'What is my gift?' Rather as a whole church we should be seeking spiritual gifts for the church, and above all, the gift of prophecy.

This immediately ties in with other verses in 1 Corinthians 12–14, which make it clear that the gifts are for the benefit of the church; they are not to satisfy our need for a gift. So Paul writes, 'Now to each one the manifestation of the Spirit is given for the common good' (12:7). Again, 'Since you are eager to have spiritual gifts, try to excel in gifts that build up the church' (14:12).

Because of the emphasis that the gifts are given to the church for the good of the whole church, it means that any member of the body may be moved on by the Holy Spirit to minister a gift at any time. I remember one Sunday visiting a church in Bristol. During the worship someone spoke in a tongue, which was followed by a most wonderful, and Christ exalting, interpretation. My wife was so impressed that she spoke to the 'interpreter' after the meeting. My wife said, 'You have a remarkable gift of interpretation of tongues.' To which the young lady replied, 'I've never done it before!' It is like that with spiritual gifts, they are for the whole body of Christ, and might be expressed by any of the church's members.

Having said that, it is also true that some believers will tend to minister a particular gift frequently and effectively. So, in my own church, I have noticed although we have many who prophesy and a number who only do so 'once in a blue moon', we do have a few who seem to have 'a gift of prophecy'.

At the end of 1 Corinthians 12, Paul asks, 'Do all work

miracles? Do all have gifts of healing? Do all speak in tongues? Do all interpret?' (vv. 29, 30). The Greek construction absolutely requires the answer 'No' to all these questions. The reverse then is obviously true. Some do work miracles, some do have gifts of healing and so on. Experience proves that this is the case.

Are the gifts genuine?

It is necessary to face this question, because even some who have theologically acknowledged the possibility of spiritual gifts are sometimes cynical about their actual operation.

There are in fact three possible 'sources' for spiritual gifts. Obviously, we expect a gift to be a genuine gift of the Spirit and when it is, it will in some measure strengthen and build up the church.

However a gift can be ministered 'in the flesh'. Someone can bring a 'prophecy' but actually it springs from their imagination and does not come by inspiration of the Spirit. How do we know when this is the case? Well, the Bible tells us to 'weigh' prophecy and a prophecy like this will not strengthen and build up the church. It will not do the church any harm. The effect will simply be neutral. This needs to be handled sensitively and privately. A leader can get alongside the person involved and counsel them to wait on God and be sure that he or she has got something from the Lord before bringing it to the church. It is probably best if such a person checks it out in the future with a leader when he or she feels they have something to bring.

Because there are genuine spiritual gifts, there are counterfeit spiritual gifts and the source of them is demonic. Some of the cults claim to use spiritual gifts. Spiritualist churches claim to have gifts of healing. The counterfeit has real power and typically tends to put people into spiritual bondage that has to be broken if they are going to become totally free in Christ.

In more than 18 years in one church where we experience spiritual gifts in nearly all our meetings, I have known only two occasions when there has been a clear manifestation of the counterfeit. When it happens it brings condemnation and fear; which is the very opposite of building up the church. When it occurred we dealt with it immediately and publicly for the security and good of the whole church.

When people tend to cynicism about spiritual gifts it will usually be around the area of healing and miracles. If someone is not convinced that there are ever genuine healings and miracles, it raises the question of how they can be sure that other gifts like prophecy or tongues and interpretation are real.

I have no doubt I have seen genuine healings. I have not seen as many as I would want to see, but I have seen the real thing, including healing from cancer. On one occasion in our church we had a lady sitting in the meeting on a Sunday morning who had suffered from severe back trouble for many years. During the meeting those who wanted prayer for healing were invited to stand while people nearby laid hands on them and prayed. The wife of one of our elders, who is not known for having a gift of healing, prayed for her. The lady found her pain levels dramatically increasing and was about to scream out for the praying to stop when all the pain went suddenly and immediately – she was healed.

Miracles are rather more difficult as people will debate exactly what constitutes a miracle. During the first phase of our church building programme we reached a point where we needed £30,000 to complete the initial purchase of the property. We called a prayer meeting that seemed to comprise almost exclusively students and the unemployed. It did not look like a £30,000 prayer meeting! The following Sunday we had an offering and raised exactly £30,000. How do hundreds of people combine their giving when they do not know what anybody else is giving, to make the exact right sum? I believe it was a miracle. Some may feel that doesn't constitute a real miracle; it was just a case of financial luck. Well, in South Africa I met a woman who died and was raised to life again after prayer. Now that is a real miracle!

I have again and again heard men and women give an accurate word of knowledge. One remarkable evening in Holy Trinity, Brompton, in London, I heard a prophet accurately call out the names of people he had never met, but which were given to him supernaturally, and say something relevant to their precise circumstances.

But how can we know that the interpretation of a tongue is the correct one? From time to time I will interpret a tongue myself. Sometimes I have been beaten to it by someone else who has brought something totally in line with what I was going to bring. The Holy Spirit seems to have confirmed the interpretation through two witnesses.

So, I have experienced more than enough to convince me that spiritual gifts are genuine. That is not to claim that every manifestation of every spiritual gift has been remarkable. But then not every sermon I have heard has been remarkable, but it has still been a sermon!

Tongues and prophecy

We are probably likely to experience these two gifts more than any other and Paul gives extended teaching on these gifts in 1 Corinthians 14.

It is helpful to notice a particular distinction between these two gifts. In 1 Corinthians 14, Paul argues again and again for the absolute necessity of an interpretation to follow a tongue, otherwise the gift is useless for building up the church. So the real question is, what is the difference between prophecy, and tongues with interpretation? The answer is clearly given in 1 Corinthians 14:2, 3: 'For anyone who speaks in a tongue does not speak to men but to God ... But everyone who prophesies speaks to men'. So we expect that when there is a tongue the interpretation will be directed towards God in some way, revealing something of his majesty or extolling his mighty works.

Prophecy will be spoken by a man or woman but will say

something to us from God. So tongues is not a prophecy with an introduction in a language we cannot understand: it is directed towards the Lord. It is difficult to understand why some debate this point, but it may be for one of two reasons.

Sometimes people speak of a message in tongues. The use of the word 'message' gives the idea that we are receiving something that way. But the phrase is unbiblical for we do not read anywhere in the New Testament of a message in tongues.

The other reason is probably because people have heard a tongue and the 'interpretation' has been in the form of a prophecy. What is probably happening here is that someone in the congregation has a genuine prophecy and when they hear a tongue they assume they have the interpretation, but actually they bring the prophecy. Occasionally, this happens in our meetings, but we still wait for the interpretation. If we feel it necessary we will give a quick word of explanation.

Apart from 14:2,3 the only other occasions in this passage where there is any hint of direction for a tongue, it is again towards God. In verses 15 and 16, Paul speaks about praying with his spirit and praising God with his spirit. This praying and praising with tongues is clearly directed towards God.

Tongues as a sign?
The following passage tends to cause a great of deal of confusion.

> Brothers, stop thinking like children. In regard to evil be infants,
> but in your thinking be adults. In the Law it is written:
> 'Through men of strange tongues
> and through the lips of foreigners
> I will speak to this people,
> but even then they will not listen to me,'
> says the Lord.
> Tongues, then, are a sign, not for believers but for unbelievers;
> prophecy however, is for believers, not for unbelievers. So if the
> whole church comes together and everyone speaks in tongues,

and some who do not understand or some unbelievers come in,
will they not say that you are out of your mind? But if an unbe-
liever or someone who does not understand comes in while every-
body is prophesying, he will be convinced by all that he is a
sinner and will be judged by all, and the secrets of his heart will
be laid bare. So he will fall down and worship God, exclaiming,
'God is really among you!' (vv. 20–25).

It is vital to grasp the fact that verse 21 with its reference to
men of strange lips introduces the rest of the passage. If not, it
stands as an isolated irrelevance in this chapter. If it is
ignored, then the rest of the passage makes no sense. The verse
is itself a quote from Isaiah 28 where mention is made of the
Assyrian invasion of Israel that brought into the nation men
who spoke in strange unintelligible languages. Therefore their
'tongues' were a sign of God's judgement on the nation. So,
when in verse 22 we read that tongues are a sign for unbelievers, it must refer to a sign of judgement, which it is certainly
not for believers.

In what sense are tongues a sign of judgement?
Unbelievers hearing tongues do not recognise the activity of
the Spirit and even declare it madness. So it is a sign that they
are not God's people, it is a sign of judgement.

It is often assumed that when it says in verse 23 that
'everyone speaks in tongues' it means that the whole church
speaks in tongues together at the same time. But that is to read
into the text more than is there. In verse 24 Paul speaks about
'everybody prophesying' but no one reads into that verse that
they were all doing it together at the same time, for that would
be ridiculous. No, Paul keeps arguing through this chapter that
tongues without interpretation is of no value.

He pictures a situation where an unbeliever comes into a
meeting and one member after another speaks in a tongue, but
it is not followed by an interpretation. The unbeliever is not a
spiritual person, he cannot recognise any spiritual activity
taking place, he does not know what is going on because he

cannot understand the language, so he concludes that everyone is out of their mind!

However, if an unbeliever comes into the meeting and everybody prophesies one by one, he is listening to something that is for the believer. But because he can understand the prophecy, which is in his own language, he may come under conviction of sin and testify, 'God is really among you!'

Fitting and orderly!

Paul's conclusion to 1 Corinthians 14 is: 'But everything should be done in a fitting and orderly way' (v. 40). I can remember when charismatic renewal began to lead to new forms of worship. Hands were being raised, people were clapping and some were beginning to dance in the meetings. This text was used to condemn such behaviour – 'everything should be done in a fitting and orderly way'.

But that is to wrench the verse out of context. What Paul is saying is that when it comes to spiritual gifts, and he has been teaching specifically on tongues and prophecy, then they should be ministered in a fitting and orderly way. That way is what he has been describing in this chapter.

Clear guidelines

There are some clear guidelines for speaking in tongues. There must be interpretation. This is so important that it is possible for the one who brings the tongue to interpret his own tongue (v. 13). In a meeting there should be no more than two or three tongues given (v. 27). If one tongue is given and there is no interpretation then there must not be another tongue (v. 28). The church must understand, so that the people can be edified (v. 5).

There are clear guidelines for prophecy. Everyone can bring a prophecy (v. 31). Only two or three prophecies should come at any one time in the meeting (v. 29). This is simply common sense, for the congregation cannot retain and cope with more than two or three prophecies at any one time. No one should dominate with a gift of prophecy (v. 30). There should be careful weighing by 'others' of what is said in a prophecy (v. 29). This is very important if there is some direction being given to the church, so that God's people are not led in the wrong direction. There is some debate about who the 'others' are that are to weigh the prophecies. But ultimately the elders of the church must be responsible here.

True, evangelical Christianity is not selective of scripture but seeks to understand and apply the whole of scripture. That is why so-called charismatic Christianity is true evangelical Christianity. There is a desire in the New Churches to take the teaching of spiritual gifts very seriously. We need the gifts of the Holy Spirit so that together as the body of Christ we can live and minister more like Jesus did. We are to eagerly desire spiritual gifts for the church so that the whole body of Christ can be strengthened and built up.

Chapter 12   # Prayer
Passion and purpose

Preach or write on the subject of prayer and one's own weaknesses in this area are immediately only too apparent. However the need for prayer has been a huge emphasis among the New Churches. Corporately, we could again lament our weakness in this area, but we know that the people of God need to pray. I once heard the well-known Bible teacher Michael Eaton say, 'A praying church is tautology. A church must pray or it is not a church.'

There have been three influences upon me that are some explanation for the material in this chapter.

Firstly, in the New Churches prayer has been a real priority. My own personal testimony is that until I crossed over into the new Restoration movement I had never been in an environment where there was a serious and sustained commitment to corporate prayer.

This is by no means to claim that it did not exist anywhere outside the New Churches, but to say that it had not been my experience. Whether in a church or college, prayer meetings were often combined with Bible studies and therefore the time of prayer was brief. Prayer meetings were often filled with embarrassed silences and there was rarely much passion expressed. Without claiming that every New Church prayer meeting is sensational I have nevertheless found myself in a different prayer environment. In general I discovered prayer meetings were longer, there was genuine passion and there were few, if any, times of silence.

Secondly, testimonies from Korea have especially shaped

our style of praying. Some years ago we began to hear stories from the huge prayer gatherings in Korea when all the people would pray together at the same time. This may well reflect the way the early church prayed. We read of one early prayer meeting: 'They raised their voices together in prayer to God. "Sovereign Lord," they said, "you made the heaven and the earth and the sea, and everything in them"' (Acts 4:24). Certainly, we realised that with everyone praying together, everybody could be fully involved.

Sometimes individuals had felt that they could not get a chance to speak out in a prayer meeting, but now they could as we all prayed together. And for those too nervous or shy to speak out in a time of prayer, now they could raise their voice alongside others and be fully involved. This style of praying seems to have been widely adopted among the New Churches, though perhaps slightly adapted.

With the enthusiasm of new converts when first introduced to praying together we did it no other way! Today, it is more common to take a subject and begin by all praying about it together, and then once the corporate praying dies away for a number of individuals to lead out in prayer. On the whole this works well and tends to keep a sense of passion and momentum in the meeting. From time to time we still need a reminder to enter whole-heartedly into a time of praying together. Originally when we began to pray like this we were taught from the text: 'the spirit is willing, but the body is weak' (Matthew 26:41). The Spirit of God in me can pray all day. It is my flesh that fights against that, and so sometimes we need to be exhorted to make the effort and keep praying.

The third influence on me is the most personal. I have had the privilege for many years to be part of the eldership team at Church of Christ the King in Brighton with Terry Virgo, who is the father figure of the Newfrontiers family of churches. For eight years I was the senior pastor of the church and therefore have worked very closely with Terry. I have witnessed his constant and unflagging zeal for prayer. We sometimes use a rather old-fashioned expression about 'a man of prayer.' That description certainly fits Terry and his personal example has always been a challenge to me as well as being hugely influential in our family of churches.

One of the fruits of that influence is the way in which all the full-time leaders (and others who can take the time) within Newfrontiers churches meet together three times a year for two days of prayer and fasting. We believe a great deal of advance and breakthrough has come as a result of those prayer gatherings, for example in new churches being planted.

There are so many scriptures that we can turn to with regard to prayer, but I will base the rest of this chapter around these words of the apostle Paul:

> *And pray in the Spirit on all occasions with all kinds of prayers and requests. With this in mind, be alert and always keep on praying for all the saints. Pray also for me, that whenever I open my mouth, words may be given to me so that I will fearlessly make known the mystery of the gospel, for which I am an ambassador in chains. Pray that I may declare it fearlessly, as I should* (Ephesians 6:18–20).

Pray with an attitude

Paul begins this short passage on prayer with the word, 'And,' but it is not the normal Greek word. If it was we could in fact ignore it and simply read 'Pray in the Spirit.' Paul is saying something very deliberate here, '*And* pray in the Spirit.' Reading back in Ephesians 6 we see that Paul has been giving instruction about putting on the whole armour of God. So the apostle seems to be saying that when it comes to Christian warfare then we need to put on the armour of God *and* we are to pray. Paul is encouraging an attitude here. Put on armour and get praying. It really highlights the truth that the Christian life is one of action and prayer. There has always been the possibility that we make it one without the other.

Some Christians are natural doers. They are full of energy and action and they always have a new project on the go. Some churches can be like that, full of activity but with the danger that God gets left out, for there is no calling on him in prayer. Other churches can be very devotional, giving themselves only to prayer as they wait for God. But what are they waiting for God to do if they are not involved in doing something themselves?

In Exodus 17 we read the story of Israel's defeat of the Amalekites. The armies of Israel led by Joshua fought the Amalekites in the valley, while Moses went up the mountain and lifted his hands in prayer, assisted by Aaron and Hur when he became tired and his hands began to droop. In defeating the enemy there was mountain work and there was valley work. There was prayer and action. In my own church we have been very committed to action but we have always tried to come with the attitude, '*and* we are really going to pray about this.'

When we were developing our new building we hit a major issue over the payment of Value Added Tax. The amount of money involved was the very considerable figure of £300,000. We believed we had a very good case for not paying the tax and we could have approached it only with action. We did act; we went to two tribunals and eventually were pressing the case right up to the House of Lords. We involved administrators and lawyers; there was plenty of action.

But we also developed a persistent attitude in prayer and again and again over the months, we called out to God to save us from having to pay this money. Now we could have approached it by prayer alone. We could have said: 'If God knows, we'll just keep praying and leave it with him.' We both acted and became very persistent in prayer. Eventually the House of Lords found against the Customs and Excise office in another case very similar to ours and so the tax office accepted our appeal as well. There was great rejoicing in the house of God!

We can see that Paul is teaching an attitude of prayer when he says, 'Be alert' (v. 18). It is easy when praying just to drift away mentally and even begin to work out the details of our bank balance or mentally to write a shopping list. We need to be alert. Sometimes simply changing our physical posture can help. Stand up, kneel, or walk around.

Even in large prayer meetings we often encourage a change of physical position to help keep us focused in prayer. Every church member can take the attitude that there really is a ministry here for him or her. Prayer is not for a few select people who are called to be intercessors, it is for the whole church to come with the attitude that whatever else we do it is 'and pray.' No one should take a low view of their involvement in the church by such statements as: 'Well I don't do anything else really, I just pray.' Get an attitude, 'I PRAY.' Anything else? What do you mean anything else – I pray!

Through all the long years of his incredible missionary work in India, William Carey's invalid sister remained confined to her home in England, but she constantly prayed. Who won the battles in India? Surely both William and his sister did; there was action and there was prayer.

By writing about the armour of God, Paul is reminding us there is a war on. There is a need for action and prayer.

Prayer in the Spirit

'And pray in the Spirit on all occasions' (v. 18). This surely suggests a dependence on the Spirit when we pray. Jude also calls on us to pray in the Spirit. Such exhortations would oppose all dead formality in prayer. This is not to say there should not be structure to our prayers. Jesus taught his disciples to pray in what we call the Lord's Prayer. This prayer was not one that Jesus expected to be constantly repeated, but rather to teach the way we should pray.

Prayer is certainly not meant to be cold, dull and formal. Sometimes I hear a reference to a 'little prayer' and the media are very fond of referring to 'special prayers' at a time of crisis. Paul does not say let us have a little prayer or even let us say a special prayer. He tells us always to pray in the Spirit. There needs to be the dynamic activity of the Holy Spirit as we pray. To pray in the Spirit would certainly include the following:

Pray in tongues
In 1 Corinthians 14:15 Paul says he will pray with his spirit. The context of this statement is praying in tongues. Speaking in tongues is a gift of the Holy Spirit according to 1 Corinthians 12, so if we pray with our spirit, if we pray in tongues, then we are dependent on the Holy Spirit to do this. The Holy Spirit will bring inspiration and illumination to our spirit as we pray.

It is important that those convinced of spiritual gifts do not just become familiar with speaking in tongues and so let it gradually fall away. No, Paul insists in 1 Corinthians 14-15 that he prays with his mind and with his spirit.

Pray with passion
In prayer there should be a dependency on the Holy Spirit and a demonstration that we are zealous for the things of God.

Jesus himself demonstrated tremendous passion in prayer. When Jesus turned the moneychangers out of the Temple we read: 'His disciples remembered that it is written, "Zeal for your house will consume me"' (John 2:17). Christ's passion was to see the Temple as a house of prayer for the nations and his zeal for that explains his actions.

Again, Christ's own passion in prayer is seen in the way that he would sometimes pray right through the night. We read of Jesus pouring himself out in prayer late in the evening in Gethsemane: 'Father, I want those you have given me to be with me where I am, and to see my glory, the glory you have given me because you loved me before the creation of the world' (John 17:24). We can feel the passion of Christ here as he prays for the disciples.

Then we have the comment from Hebrews: 'During the days of Jesus' life on earth, he offered up prayers and petitions with loud cries and tears to the one who could save him from death, and he was heard because of his reverent submission' (Hebrews 5:7). Jesus did not pray quiet, formal prayers. There was intense zeal and passion being expressed as he cried out to the Father.

We can also see how passionate Paul must have been in prayer when he writes:

> *I speak the truth in Christ – I am not lying, my conscience confirms it in the Holy Spirit – I have great sorrow and unceasing anguish in my heart. For I could wish that I myself were cursed and cut off from Christ for the sake of my brothers, those of my own race, the people of Israel (Romans 9:1–4).*

Then he follows it up by saying:

> *Brothers, my heart's desire and prayer to God for the Israelites is that they may be saved (Romans 10:1).*

We are reading here of a man who, praying in the Spirit, prays with intense passion.

Pray with urgency
Some years ago at Stoneleigh Bible Week, Ken Gott from Sunderland preached a message with the arresting title 'The shout that stopped God.' When blind Bartimaeus heard that Jesus was in his city he began to shout out: 'Jesus, Son of David, have mercy on me!' We sometimes find it awkward and embarrassing to cope with other people's spiritual passion and so it is not a great surprise that the crowds tried to shut him up. But then Bartimaeus called out to Jesus even more urgently. Mark 10:49 says: 'Jesus stopped'! There was a shout that stopped God. In the New Churches I hear a lot of urgent praying that God will stop in a particular town or city. Certainly, we know our need of that in Brighton.

We can see the urgency of Bartimaeus. Jesus calls him, and

we read: 'Throwing his cloak aside, he jumped to his feet and came to Jesus' (v. 50). His urgency is expressed in three ways. He gets rid of a distraction – his cloak. He jumps up – this man is really pushing to get to Jesus. He shows faith – he comes to Jesus. Our urgency in prayer will be demonstrated as we get rid of distractions, really push hard to get to Jesus and come in faith. 'And without faith it is impossible to please God, because anyone who comes to him must believe that he exists and that he rewards those who earnestly seek him' (Hebrews 11:6).

All kinds of prayer

'And pray in the Spirit on all occasions with all kinds of prayers and requests.' All kinds of prayers can include long prayers and short prayers. We must rid ourselves of the idea that long prayers will always be in the Spirit, but short prayers will not be in the Spirit – sometimes it may be the other way around! Nehemiah gives us an example here. In Nehemiah 1:4–11 we read that he fasted and prayed for several days concerning the state of the devastated city of Jerusalem. These verses also include quite a long extract from his praying. But in chapter 2 when Nehemiah appears as a cupbearer before the king with a sad face, the king asks why he looks so sad. When Nehemiah tells him, the king asks him what he wants. Here is what we read: 'Then I prayed to the God of heaven, and I answered the king' (Nehemiah 2:4–5). Evidently, this was not a long season of prayer. It can scarcely have been more than, 'God help me', but it was effective. Sometimes the only kind of prayer we have time for is one breathed out in just a couple of seconds.

Another kind of prayer is prayer with fasting. Fasting is not commanded in the New Testament, but to some extent it is assumed. Jesus said: 'When you fast, do not look sombre as the hypocrites do' (Matthew 6:16). In the New Churches fasting is certainly not commanded but it is encouraged from time to time.

I have already mentioned the two days of prayer and fasting that Newfrontiers leaders attend three times a year.

Sometimes in our own church we will have a week of prayer and there have been times when we have encouraged our people to consider fasting for at least some of that time. This can have some other benefits when we do it in the first week of the New Year, just after Christmas! However, it is important to point out the difference between fasting and dieting. We fast in order to give time to God. I have known believers who have claimed to be on a fast and spent every mealtime watching television instead of eating. That definitely falls into the category of dieting.

40 days

Some years ago many churches believed that God was calling them to a 40-day season of prayer and fasting. Two elders in my church actually went the full 40 days without food, but most of the members took part in some way during the 40-day season. Some went on a 'Daniel' fast, eating only vegetables. Some fasted for one day each week of the 40 days, some went without lunch every day. Some fasted from television. But it was definitely a special time when the whole body was seeking God in prayer. Having said that, it is good to remember what Isaiah prophesied: 'Is not this the kind of fasting I have chosen: to loose the chains of injustice and untie the cords of the yoke, to set the oppressed free and break every yoke? Is it not to share your food with the hungry and to provide the poor wanderer with shelter ...' (Isaiah 58:6–7). There is a temptation towards pride when we fast. God makes it clear that he wants to see social justice rather than a religious ritual. This is one of the reasons why it is so important to understand the kingdom of God (see chapter 17) and not see our faith as just doing religious things.

All kinds of prayer have included big prayer meetings and the encouragement for believers to pray regularly in twos and threes.

I have to confess some dislike for the term 'prayer meeting'; it can sound so formal and religious. What we are really saying is that churches can do nothing effective without God. We meet to cry out to God for his presence and blessing. All kinds of prayer include praying for our church, for our city, for the leaders of our nation and for the unreached parts of the world. All kinds of prayer include times of adoring God, times of passionate intercession and even times when we can do little more than groan as we confront the needs of this world, but the Spirit helps us in our weakness (Romans 8:26).

Isaiah says, 'I have posted watchmen on your walls, O Jerusalem; they will never be silent day or night. You who call on the Lord, give yourselves no rest, and give him no rest till he establishes Jerusalem and makes her the praise of the earth' (Isaiah 62:6,7). The need of our nation is so great and the living church is still so small. The church must pray to see God establish his people with effectiveness and success for the good of our nation. God helps us in our weakness, but we must pray.

Chapter 13   # Money
Treasure in heaven

It has been calculated that fifteen per cent of Jesus' teaching was on the theme of money.

We all have some money. 'Not a lot', we may protest, but we all have some. The New Churches have gained some reputation for an ability to raise very large sums of money. Does this mean that they preach a prosperity doctrine? In a way the answer could be, 'yes', but the emphasis is on prosperity in eternity. Interestingly we find that the subject of money in the New Testament is often linked to another subject relevant for everyone, and that is death.

Eternity in our spirit

Although the subject of this chapter is money, it is important to see the New Testament context and to view money in the light of death and eternity.

Our songs and prayers consistently celebrate victory over death. We are going to heaven; we are going to live forever.

> *When we've been there a thousand (or ten thousand,*
>   *or ten million) years,*
> *Bright shining as the sun,*
> *We've no less days to sing God's praise*
> *Than when we've first begun.*

But let's ask the question; have we got eternity in our spirit? Jesus wanted us to have that. 'Do not store up for yourselves treasures on earth, where moth and rust destroy, and where thieves break in and steal. But store up for yourselves treasures in heaven ...' (Matthew 6:19, 20).

It is clear from Scripture that we will not just conquer death, but that we will live forever. This, according to Jesus, should cause us to think very carefully about the way we use our money now.

It is not surprising therefore that Paul says to Timothy, 'Command those who are rich in this present world not to be arrogant nor to put their hope in wealth, which is so uncertain, but to put their hope in God, who richly provides us with everything for our enjoyment' (1 Timothy 6:17). God did not give us life and creation as things to despise like the ascetics of the early church often did; he gave us a life and a world to enjoy right now.

Early on in church history there was a monk called Baradatus. To deny himself, in an extreme way, which was a common practice of those early monks, he had himself locked in a slatted wooden box. The box was open to the elements and Baradatus' bishop became anxious about his health and eventually persuaded him to come out. But Baradatus was determined not to enjoy himself. He was sewn into an animal skin with a tiny breathing hole around his mouth and nose and then lived outside in the desert, to bake in the day and freeze at night. He was a combination of a freeze-dried, boil-in-the-bag monk.

God has given us life and creation to enjoy. But there is a matter of emphasis here. We are only here for a limited time; we are 'aliens and strangers in the world' (1 Peter 2:11). We are on a visit to this world at the present time, and we have not got permanent residence. Beyond death we will live forever, so eternity needs to be in our spirit. That is why Jesus counters the popular view that we should be laying up treasures on the earth; for they will only help us for a very limited time. Rather, we should store up our treasures in heaven where they will assist us forever. The Bible always speaks common sense!

One way to tell if eternity is in our spirit, is if we are preparing for it. Many people have retirement in their spirit and prepare for it very diligently. There is no shortage of advice and aid to help us to prepare for a financially secure retirement. Certainly, that must be good as far as it goes, but there are some risks. For one thing, we may not even reach retirement.

Jesus made this clear in another money and death link when he told the parable of the rich man and his barns. The man had enough invested in his barns to give him the confidence that he could enjoy many years of ease and security. But God demanded his soul the day he retired!

I know, myself, of a man who had planned and invested carefully for a long and happy retirement. The first day of this new stage of life came and there was a heavy snowfall. He went outside to shovel the snow away from his drive, suffered a massive heart attack and died.

Of course, many men and women do reach retirement age and it may well be a happy stage of life and they may have many such years. The enjoyment of those years can certainly be helped by good planning and investment beforehand. But if we reach retirement the clock is definitely ticking. It is not so much that retirement teaches us time is running out, but that we are running out of time. What happens then?

So I am not making a tirade against pension planning, but rather standing with the Bible in suggesting we need a greater plan; a plan for eternity. Then the clock will never be against us. Richard Baxter observes: 'If there be so certain and glorious a rest for the saints, why is there no more industrious seeking after it? One would think, if a man did but once hear of such unspeakable glory to be obtained, and believed what he heard to be true, he should be transported with the vehemency of his desire after it, and should care for nothing else, and speak of and inquire after nothing else, but how to get this treasure. And yet people who hear of it daily, and profess to believe it as a fundamental article of their faith, do as little mind it, or labour for it, as if they had never heard of any such thing or did not believe one word they hear."[1]

So there is a very pertinent question we should ask ourselves. Is eternity in our spirit?

Preparing for the long tomorrow

This life gives us a window of opportunity to prepare for eternity. Nicholas van Hoogstraten has become famous in Brighton, the city where I live, for attempting to build the largest house in England during the last century. The building operations were somewhat interrupted when Mr Hoogstraten was sentenced to ten years in prison. However, his avowed intention is to be buried in the house when he dies, surrounded by the purchases of his multi-million pound fortune. These material possessions are to be held in a trust that will never allow them to be sold and to benefit anyone else.

The reality is that we cannot take it with us when we go, although the Bible makes it clear that we can send it on ahead of us. There is an uncertainty about life at all times and we will not all reach 70 years of age. But many do reach 70 and indeed these days many live on into their 80s and 90s. I remember the day that the late Queen Mother reached her 100th birthday and publicly opened her special birthday card from her daughter, the Queen. I was surprised to read that another twelve U.K. citizens also received such a birthday card from the Queen on the same day. People can live to a great age these days.

But none of us can halt the passing of the years and even to live for 100 years is still a short period compared with the great sweep of history and of course as nothing viewed against the background of eternity. It is quite likely that in just two or three generations even our direct descendants will know nothing about us. I certainly know nothing at all about any of my great-grandparents. History sweeps on.

However, right now, we have the opportunity to invest for our certain eternity. What we do now will have an effect on our eternity. The key idea behind Jesus' call in Matthew 6 not to store up treasure on earth, but in heaven, is that of investment. You can easily find a Financial Advisor who will help you to plan for your retirement – if you reach it. Jesus gives us advice about planning for eternity which we will certainly reach and where the investment will definitely pay out.

There is plenty of teaching in scripture about those who invested for their future. Abraham did: 'By faith Abraham, when called to go to a place he would later receive as his inheritance, obeyed and went, even though he did not know where he was going ... For he was looking forward to the city with foundations, whose architect and builder is God' (Hebrews 11:8,10).

Moses did: 'He (Moses) regarded disgrace for the sake of Christ as of greater value than the treasures of Egypt, because he was looking ahead to his reward' (Hebrews 11:26).

Jesus did: 'Let us fix our eyes on Jesus, the author and perfecter of our faith, who for the joy set before him endured the cross, scorning its shame, and sat down at the right hand of the throne of God' (Hebrews 12 :2). The joy set before Jesus was the church that would be his. He invested his life, despising shame and agony to gain the church as the joy of his reward.

'Without a doubt, the single greatest contribution to our inability to see money and possessions in their true light is our persistent failure to see our present lives through the lens of eternity' (Randy Alcorn).[2] In 1 Corinthians 3 vv. 10–15 Paul writes about the need to build well on the foundation of Christ that has been laid in our lives. It is possible to enter heaven, the apostle tells us, truly saved 'but only as one escaping through the flames'. Whether we have built well in our Christian lives will partly be assessed by the way we have invested our money. Our use of money will, I believe, affect the gain or loss of reward as we enter heaven. So have we really got eternity in our spirit?

Jesus warns us in Matthew 6 against putting our hope in earthly treasures and investments. For one thing, earthly investments are always relatively poor investments. They are certainly not evil; they just have a limited pay-off for a few years on the earth.

Also they are uncertain. Jesus speaks in terms of their vulnerability to moth, rust and theft. Today, we know that stock markets fall, interest rates on savings can be very low and that pension schemes can collapse. Earthly investments are a worry – they can lose their value. And they can be a distraction, for Jesus tells us, 'For where your treasure is, there your heart will be also' (Matthew 6 :21).

Philip Yancey writes: 'I feel pulled in opposite directions over the money issue. Sometimes I want to sell all I own, join a Christian commune and live out my days in intentional poverty. At other times I want to rid myself of guilt and enjoy the fruits of our nation's prosperity. Mostly, I wish I did not have to think about it at all. But I must come to terms with the Bible's very strong statements about money.'[3] We can probably sympathise with those different feelings. However, that does not relieve us from the responsibility of good investment right now.

The pay-off

A friend once wrote this to me: 'If we look at God's example in giving, we have a vital key to our financial management. He gave, expecting something in return. In Christ, he gave regardless of the cost, so that he could redeem mankind for himself and give his Beloved many children. He "sowed" a Son so that he could reap many sons. He always gives for a purpose and always so that he will receive grateful worship. Therefore we too must give in faith, expecting him to give in return. I have heard the opposite taught; give, not because we expect to receive. While this sounds good and moral it does not appear to be scriptural.'

I essentially agree with this because I believe that the Bible teaches us to invest our money. We expect a return from investments. The question is, when do we get the payback, if we are investing in the kingdom of God? Well, there is some payback in the present time. 'But seek first his kingdom and his righteousness and all these things will be given to you as well' (Matthew 6:33). We can be seeking God's kingdom in the way we use our money, and the above verse, understood in its context, means that God will supply for our present material needs. However, God does not promise to provide for our self-ishly motivated greed.

In 2 Corinthians 9 Paul is teaching about generous giving of our money and he also promises a payback at the present time. 'You will be made rich in every way so that you can be generous on every occasion ...' (v. 11). Here the return on our generous investing in God's work is to enable us to give even more generously to God's work!

But even more than a reward now, for our investing in God's kingdom, is the promise of reward in eternity to come. In Luke 16 Jesus tells a parable about the shrewd use of money. He then makes this extraordinary statement: 'I tell you, use worldly wealth to gain friends for yourselves, so that when it is gone, you will be welcomed into eternal dwellings' (v. 9). We do not really expect to hear Jesus telling us to use money to win friendship but we need to note the emphasis on eternal dwellings here.

We can generously give money today to support the work of God. Such giving can help promote the church's mission, outreach and planting. In eternity we will then be welcomed into heaven by those saved through the work of the church. There will be a direct link between the money we have given and the salvation of those we have never known on the earth but who certainly want to be our friends in heaven. That will be a great reward from our investment.

How much?

This brings us to the question of how much should we invest into God's work? We can feel frustrated by our own limited resources and therefore the restricted opportunities to give. For those who have very little, Luke's story of the widow's mite can be a real challenge, although it should also be a challenge for those blessed with large financial resources. The poor widow gave everything she had into the Temple treasury. Does that mean, even though we may have very little, that we should give everything into the church offering? Personally, I believe that the lesson we should draw from this story is that what appears to be very little can be a lot – it was a lot for the widow – in fact for her it was everything. But the reverse must also be true. What appears a lot can be very little.

I want to put this into the context of tithing. Many evangelical churches teach tithing: that is giving ten per cent of our income to the work of God. The Jewish Law required a tithe from the people of Israel, but the danger here is that we make tithing a law for people to whom we want to teach grace. Legalism always achieves something, but usually it achieves the minimum rather than the maximum.

If you tithe on an income of £100 you give £10. If you tithe on an income of £1000 you give £100. But surely the real issue is not how much is given, but how much is left. To tithe £1000 leaves you with £900, whereas to tithe £100 could mean you are left really struggling on only £90.The New Testament teaches very strongly in such chapters as 2 Corinthians 8 and 9 that we should give generously. It does not take us back to the law of tithing. For some to give £10 from £100 may be very generous giving whereas £100 from £1000 could be downright stingy.

Some say Jesus did mention tithing, giving apparent approval to those who tithed herbs and spices (Luke 11:42). This hardly seems to stand as a convincing proof text in contrast to the broader teaching on generosity. And who is bothering to tithe the mint in their garden today, anyway, even if they teach that money should be tithed?

It is true that both Abraham and Jacob, who lived before the Law, gave God ten per cent of all they had. But when we study the relevant passages in Genesis chapters 14 and 28 we see that it was a freely given offering, not one demanded by law. It might be a good example, but it does not establish a rule.

Randy Alcorn writes: 'What does it mean to lay up treasure

in heaven instead of on earth? It means that Christ offers us the incredible opportunity to trade earthly goods and currency for eternal kingdom rewards. By putting our money and possessions in his treasury, we assure ourselves of eternal rewards beyond comprehension.'[4]

John Bunyan once said: 'Whatever good thing you do for him, if done according to the word, is laid up for you in treasure chests and coffers to be brought out to be recorded before both men and angels, to your eternal comfort.'[5] Again, we have an encouragement to invest for eternity. Generosity now will mean a rich reward in heaven.

There is a great temptation to store up for ourselves treasures upon the earth and the pressure of advertising and our desire for future security is strongly upon us to do that. Christ's call is to store up treasures in heaven, where we will receive eternal rewards.

Have we got eternity in our spirit? Do our investments reveal it? Do we have a spirit of generosity in our giving? The church of God needs vast sums of money to help her in her mission. The people of God are able to give a lot of money, but inferior investing will hold back the church's advance. That will mean the church's mission is also held back. There was no greater act of generosity than God giving us his Son for our salvation. That sets the example. Generous giving by the people of God is the best financial investment we can make.

Notes
1. *The Saints' Everlasting Rest*, Richard Baxter, Grand Rapids, Mich., Baker, 1981, pp. 39–40.
2. *Money, Possessions and Eternity*, Randy Alcorn, Tyndale, 1989, p. 138.
3. *Money*, Philip Yancey, Portland, Multnomah Press, 1985, p. 3.
4. *Money, Possessions and Eternity*, Randy Alcorn, Tyndale, 1989, p. 127.
5. Quoted by Bruce Wilkinson in the 'Walk Thru Eternal Rewards' seminar notebook, Atlanta Ga., Walk Thru the Bible Ministries.

Chapter 14   # Marriage
Ordained by God

In many of the New Churches there is a lot of attention given to teaching on marriage. Restored churches want to demonstrate good role models here to inspire future generations.

The subject of marriage is very often dealt with topically. We see publicity for seminars with titles like: 'How to improve your marriage' or 'Ten vital keys to a good marriage'.

There is obviously a place for doing this. But I want to consider marriage directly out of the Bible and essentially from the longest passage on the subject in the fifth chapter of Ephesians.

It is important to address this subject, in a book whose emphasis is on restoring the church to a biblical pattern, because of today's drift away from marriage. If marriage is something that is taught in God's Word then it needs to be demonstrated most thoroughly, and indeed attractively, in the church. I find today, that each time I fill in a form that has a requirement for me to disclose some personal details, there will be a line that says: Name of Partner, never today, Name of Husband/Wife. That certainly is an adjustment to what has happened in our society. In church settings we try as much as possible to avoid the term 'partner' and speak of a husband or wife.

Sadly, marriages in the world are breaking down at an alarming rate, but also divorces among Christians and even Christian leaders these days are by no means unknown. During the 1970s and 80s I led a church of 200 members for ten years and there was not one single marriage breakdown in the church during that time. This would certainly not be typical in a church, only a few years later, at the beginning of the 21st century.

It is very important that single believers also know God's teaching on this subject. For one thing they may themselves be married one day and even if not, what God has ordained ought to be understood and honoured by the whole body of Christ.

Mutual submission

'Wives, submit to your husbands as to the Lord' (Ephesians 5:22). I have been told by members of my church who attended a large evangelical conference that when this verse was read during one of the meetings there were members of the congregation that hissed in disapproval. That is definitely the spirit of the age getting into the church. In fact it is vital to see that this passage of scripture really begins in the previous verse. Verse 21 says, 'Submit to one another out of reverence for Christ.' Paul then goes on to cover three areas of relationships where such submission needs to be shown: in marriage, in family life and in the workplace.

In a general sense the submission required here means seeking the best for the functioning and health of the relationship. So the exhortation for wives to submit to their husbands essentially means that they should seek the highest good and progress in their relationship with their husband. But the husband is to care for his wife and seek her highest good also. In that sense there is to be mutual submission. But of course there is not only mutual submission, for in verse 23 we are told that the husband is head of the wife. Here is an extremely important principle: *mutual submission requires leadership*.

South Africa uses a four-way stop system on their roads. If cars are approaching a crossroads then the cars are to cross in the order that they arrive. The first car to arrive goes ahead first and so on. Now suppose four cars arrive at the four different exits to the junction at exactly the same time. Who goes first? Well there actually needs to be some submission here, because if all cars move off together then they will crash in the middle of the junction. But what happens if they all submit to one another with every car driver waiting for the other car driver to move off first? You can argue that there is mutual submission, but also a total stalemate because no one moves! The fact is, mutual submission demands leadership. And God knows that.

So, in a marriage relationship where there is a call to mutual submission, God gives leadership to the man, both to avoid collision and conflict on every issue, but also to avoid stagnation and indecision within the marriage.

These verses from Ephesians 5 really test our attitude towards the Bible.

There can be rebellion
We can take the attitude that we will not obey a scripture that tells wives to submit. But such resistance is not to a preacher or a church, but rather to God who is the author of his Word.

There can be manipulation
We can accept that this is what the Bible says, but then make the point that it was said in a very different time from ours. We can claim to live in a radically different culture from the setting of the New Testament, times have changed and therefore this scripture is not really relevant for today.

There is a real danger here that we manipulate the Bible. We need to consider that 2000 years ago a wife was treated as a possession and that divorce was endemic in Roman, Greek and Jewish societies. There were some rabbis who taught that something as trivial as a wife providing a badly cooked meal was a possible trigger for a divorce. Indeed at the most extreme it was suggested that even the desire for a younger and prettier wife was a good enough reason to divorce your present wife. It is against that background that we need to see that Paul was not a man of his time as is so often expressed. For Paul to teach that a husband should love his wife just as Christ loved the church (v. 25) was a revolutionary approach for those days.

There can be acceptance
Acceptance of this scripture must not be made with a resigned sort of attitude – well that's what the Bible says and I suppose that I just have to accept it. Rather we need in accepting this scripture to try really to understand what it means and also how it is to be applied.

We note therefore this important principle that mutual submission requires leadership.

The mystery of marriage

In verse 32 Paul speaks of 'a profound mystery'. But what is he talking about? He says that he is talking about Christ and the church. However, from the previous verse it is also clear that he is talking about two people becoming one flesh in marriage – this is also a profound mystery. Those of us who are married could perhaps identify with our marriage being described in terms of a profound mystery! However we also need to realise that in the New Testament the word 'mystery' can be used of something previously hidden and now revealed. So, do we have the revelation about marriage? We will look at this in terms of union and celebration.

Union
'For this reason a man will leave his father and mother and be united to his wife, and the two will become one flesh' (v. 31). The reference to one flesh is clearly a reference to sexual union, but to more than that. In sexual union two people give themselves to one another in the most complete and intimate way possible. This is why it needs to be in the context of marriage, for there needs to be security for such intimacy.

To be 'one flesh' involves a whole life together. A man and a woman talk together, share together, dream together, eat together, sleep together and often have children as a result of being together. It is their whole lives together that make two people one flesh. So a husband and wife are united together in a total sense and there is therefore a profound mystery. Mathematically it means the 1+1=1 and not 2.

There is revelation as we realise that this union speaks also of the relationship between Christ and the church. There is a total belonging together, a union that cannot be broken. The quality and integrity of the relationship between Christ and the church is best illustrated in human terms in the union of marriage. One flesh speaks of the relationship between Christ and the church.

It is important to see marriage like that, for it gives it such a sense of dignity and purpose. If a marriage is full of squabbles and lack of communication, or if there is deceit, or cheating or unkindness, grumbling against one another or public 'put downs' then it will not demonstrate what it is meant to. In a marriage two believers are united as one flesh to give a tangible demonstration of the relationship between Christ and the church.

Celebration

A marriage involves celebration. A man and a woman leave their parental homes, or as often happens within our culture, they leave their parents as the primary relationship even if they have already left home. Now there is to be a new primary relationship between this husband and wife. So as well as union there is a celebration of this new relationship. This celebration both points to and reflects the wedding of the Lamb.

In verse 27 we read that Christ presents to himself a radiant church, which in context is also understood as a radiant bride. It may seem strange that Christ presents the bride to himself, for usually the father presents the bride to the bridegroom. But Christ has purchased this bride with his blood and so only he has the right to present the bride to himself.

This presentation is described in the Book of Revelation:

Then I heard what sounded like a great multitude, like the roar of rushing waters and like loud peals of thunder, shouting:

'Hallelujah! For our Lord God Almighty reigns. Let us rejoice and be glad and give him glory! For the wedding of the Lamb has come, and his bride has made herself ready' (19:6,7).

So this is a great celebration and all weddings should reflect that joy. A wedding does not have to be expensive to be an occasion of great joy and celebration. So many couples these days are far too worried about making an impression at the wedding rather than giving attention to the much more important matter of preparing for the marriage.

But think of the bride that Christ has purchased. She has been washed and made perfect by the blood of Christ. The angels bear witness to the wedding of the Lamb; the joining together of the church and Jesus Christ, who will enjoy unrestricted fellowship and intimacy forever. Every problem will have gone. Every tear will have been wiped away. What Jesus came to do in his saving work will be fully consummated. The full number of the redeemed will be gathered in.

What a bride! What a bridegroom! What an extraordinary home will be established for them when the whole universe is rearranged in a new heaven and earth. What an amazing wedding, and what a glorious marriage. There will be an eternity-long celebration. This is the truth about Christ and the church.

Making it happen

What are the practical ways that demonstrate the reality of mutual submission and such a profound mystery?

Husbands
'Husbands, love your wives, just as Christ loved the church and gave himself up for her to make her holy, cleansing her by the washing with water through the word' (vv. 25–26). This appeal to husbands to love their wives is set at the very highest level; it is not just that Christ gave himself for the church, but he

gave himself *up* for her. There was a total surrender; for Christ gave all.

This is how a husband is to love his wife. In Hebrews we read, 'Let us fix our eyes on Jesus, the author and perfecter of our faith, who for the joy set before him endured the cross, scorning its shame, and sat down at the right hand of the throne of God' (12:2). Jesus held nothing back to purchase the church. He plumbed the depths of hell at Calvary. There was the most agonising pain and the terrible humiliation of public shame that was the awful cost of bearing sin. He put himself where we should have been; under the wrath of God. Christ endured all of that. He gave himself up for his bride. No higher price will ever be paid for a bride; but Christ paid it in full.

There is a sense in which Christ is still giving himself for the bride. He is cleaning her up and this is a continuing process.

...Christ loved the church and gave himself up for her to make her holy, cleansing her by washing of water through the word, and to present her to himself as a radiant church, without stain or wrinkle or any other blemish, but holy and blameless (Ephesians 5:25–27).

These are not easy verses to understand but would indicate that whereas baptism in water marks our initial cleansing from sin, so the process of keeping the bride clean comes through application of the word of God. As it says in John 17:17, 'Sanctify them by the truth; your word is truth.' So even now Christ is concerned for his people. This sets an example that means that husbands should have a continuing love for their wives (Ephesians 5:28). How in practical terms is this to be done?

The husband's responsibilities

Counting through the words of this passage I calculate that while 58 words are addressed directly to the wife, exactly twice as many, 116 words, are addressed directly to the husband!

Husbands should be constant lovers

'For the husband is the head of the wife as Christ is the head of the church, his body, of which he is the Saviour' (v. 23). How can the husband be the 'saviour' of his wife? In 1 Timothy 4:10 we read that God is the Saviour of all men, especially of those who believe. He is the Saviour of all men in the more general sense of being the Preserver of all men and women who are alive on the earth. Nobody could draw a single breath without God preserving him or her. So a husband should be the saviour of his wife in the sense that he really looks after her, he is her constant lover. This is not to be according to a passing mood, but he is to be always concerned to care for her.

The Roman Catholic Church still requires a celibate priest-hood. We may have criticisms of this, but behind it is the belief that a man should be free to devote himself in an undistracted way to the care of the church. It is recognition, at one level, that if you have a wife you need to give her your care and attention, and that will lessen your opportunity to give time and attention to the church. A wife needs time, but more than just time, real loving attention.

Paul Tournier, the famous Christian counsellor tells the story of how a woman complained to him that her husband was a 'mysterious island'![1] So the husband needs to do more than simply be there, giving his wife time in a passive way, he needs to communicate.

A sacrificial lover

'Husbands, love your wives, just as Christ loved the church and gave himself up for her' (v. 25). John Chrystostom the 'golden-mouthed' preacher of early church history commenting on this passage said, 'Have you seen the measure of obedience? Hear also the measure of love. Would you that your wife should obey you as the church does Christ? Have care for her yourself as Christ for the church. And if it be needful that you should give your life for her, or be cut to pieces a thousand times, or endure anything whatsoever, refuse it not – He brought the church to his feet by his great care, not by threats nor fear nor any such thing. So you conduct yourself towards your wife.'[2]

A Christian husband is a lover, not a tyrant. A wife can submit to a husband who demonstrates sacrificial love towards her. The domination of a wife by a husband is not a biblical doctrine, but a personal moral failure. So a husband is to be sacrificial in his care for his wife, but is also prepared to give a lead and then to take the responsibility for that leadership. This is the way of love.

An attentive lover

Christ is an attentive lover. 'In this same way, husbands ought to love their wives as their own bodies. He who loves his wife loves himself. After all, no-one ever hated his own body, but he feeds and cares for it, just as Christ does the church' (vv. 28–29). A man will usually be very careful to look after himself. He knows what he wants to eat; he will make sure that he gets the right amount of sleep and leisure. As we sometimes say, he looks after number one. But does he give his wife the same attention, for of course, husband and wife are one.

This is again very practical. Does the husband really understand how much money a wife may need each week to buy food for the family? I find it very instructive, and somewhat sobering, to do the food shopping with my wife sometimes, and discover how much everything really costs. If there are young children in the family, is the husband giving his wife the help she really needs here? Does the husband make sure, when there is a church meeting on, and one of them needs to stay at home to look after the children, that he really considers what meetings will be a blessing to his wife? He doesn't just send her out because he wants an evening off! A husband who is an attentive lover will pray with his wife and for his wife.

Husbands are to love their wives as Christ loves the church. There is to be a submission of the husband to the wife in his willingness to care for her and to love her with sacrificial attention. This also helps to demonstrate the profound mystery of marriage.

The wife's responsibilities

'Wives, submit to your husbands as to the Lord' (v. 22). I have seen congregations look rather astonished when I have told them that the word 'submit' does not appear here in the Greek text. But it is important not to get too excited about this! The word 'submit' does appear in the previous verse. It is a common device in writing the Greek language not to write down the same verb twice in two successive phrases. So if a verb appears in the first phrase, but not in the second phrase, then it is understood that you carry the verb from the first phrase into the next one.

The same rule applies in verse 24 where we read that the church submits to Christ and so also wives should submit to their husbands. Although the second 'submit' is absent in the Greek text we must understand from the previous phrase that it means that wives should submit to their husbands. This does enable us to say, however, that there is no heavy underlining of the word 'submit' for both verses 22 and 24 point out that a wife's submission to her husband is to reflect the church's submission to Christ. The church submits voluntarily to Christ, because she knows she is loved and wants to respond to him in love.

In a good marriage the issue of submission is not a matter of daily concern. The husband will not be thinking, 'Have I had ten good submissions today'! The wife will not be constantly anxious about whether she has submitted enough. However there are times in every marriage when a decision has to be made and yet there is a genuine difference of opinion between husband and wife. If after talking and praying it through there is still no agreement, then it is for the husband to take the lead and make the decision.

He also carries the responsibility for that decision and certainly should not then blame his wife if things do not work out as he had hoped. The alternatives to this are either that the issue becomes a matter of conflict between husband and wife or that they simply do not make any decision and remain in limbo on the issue. The fact that in such a situation the husband can take the lead and carry the responsibility should actually take pressure off his wife.

Should such submission by the wife be unconditional? Certainly not if the wife's conscience is violated or she is asked to disobey God. There is a final authority that is higher than that of any husband. But if the husband is seeking to love his wife as Christ loves the church, if he is a lover and not a tyrant, then a wife should be able to submit to her husband's lead with confidence and love.

Christian marriage

We live in a very self-centred age and society. Many married couples run the danger of being introspective and focused only on their own needs in their marriage. A Christian couple needs to keep their relationship God-focused so that it can be a valid demonstration of the relationship between Christ and his church. Such a focus and desire could be a remedy for many 'needs' within the marriage anyway.

A Christian marriage can have evangelistic impact. As we live in a society where there is a continuing meltdown in relationships, a strong marriage can be a real provocation. It can really show something of the wonderful relationship between Christ and his church.

Notes
1. *Marriage Difficulties*, Paul Tournier, SCM Press, 1968, p. 16.
2. *The Letters to the Galatians and Ephesians*, William Barclay, Daily Study Bible, The Saint Andrew Press, 1966, p. 206.

Chapter 15   Family
Building blocks

A vision and desire to see the church restored to the full biblical expression, of what the body of Christ should be, is not demonstrated by attending a lot more meetings. Indeed it is possible to be so committed to the structures and the programmes of the church that we begin to neglect our own family. Following the teaching of the New Testament, we see how a restored church will be one in which there are excellent marriages and good family life. We have plenty of instruction in the Bible to help us with this.

To write about family life and children can be a hazardous occupation. It is very easy to be full of wisdom ahead of the game, but it is probably more profitable to offer some wisdom after a time of reflection when we have played the game. I am fortunate to be the father of two sons who have married Christian wives and they are all going on with God. The next generation, in the shape of several grandchildren, is now on the scene. Preachers and writers need to be aware that sharing endless illustrations of grandchildren, which they may feel are positively delightful, does not usually carry the same force to listeners and readers!

I recall a cartoon where a pastor in his first church shares with the congregation: 'As my college principal used to say'. In his second and third pastorates there were many illustrations beginning with: 'And in my previous church'. Towards the end of his ministry the illustrations began, 'My granddaughter did the cutest thing the other day'.

But as we look at the scriptures, in the context of wanting

to build churches that really make a statement of what a people of faith look like, what do we believe about bringing up children?

The Bible teaches us in every aspect of life and here is an important statement on family life given by the apostle Paul:

> *Children, obey your parents in the Lord, for this is right. 'Honour your father and mother' – which is the first commandment with a promise – 'that it may go well with you and that you may enjoy a long life on the earth.' Fathers, do not exasperate your children; instead, bring them up in the training and instruction of the Lord (Ephesians 6:1–4).*

There will be readers of this book who are not parents. Some will be parents in the future but every Christian should have a view on the crucial matter of family life. With the breakdown of the family unit that is taking place in our society, we may sometimes be in settings where we have an opportunity to bring a biblical perspective even if we do not have children ourselves.

What Paul teaches at the beginning of Ephesians 6 is actually part of the outworking of the command: 'Be filled with the Spirit' that we read back in chapter 5 and verse 18. What does a Spirit-filled life look like? Paul tells us as he gives instruction on worship, thanksgiving and relationships. In the area of relationships, he gives teaching on marriage, family and then work. Here we are picking up on family life: the responsibilities of children to parents and then of parents to their children.

Children to parents

'Children, obey your parents in the Lord, for this is right.' Does Paul mean here that the children are 'in the Lord', that is, they are Christian children or does he mean obeying parents is the way you obey the Lord? Probably the reference is to Christian children, for as believers, they should be living a Spirit-filled life. This is not only relevant for Christian children of Christian parents, but Christian children of non-believing parents.

What is right
The first thing that Paul says about children obeying parents is that it is right. The Bible gives us practical and common sense instruction. Why should children obey their parents? Because it is the right thing to do. This is the natural order of things recognised in all cultures and societies. There are certain issues in life where we never have to be unsure. There is a simple natural order. This is right.

It does not of course mean that the parents are always right. Children pass through different stages. Small children can believe that their parents know everything, but doubts quickly creep in. By the time a child is a teenager, he or she can believe their parents know nothing! Christian children have to face up to this. Their obedience is required even when their opinion on an issue may differ from that of their parents. That is true for the child of a non-believing parent as long as what the parent requires is not immoral or illegal.

In our own church we have always encouraged teenage children to obey their non-believing parents even over the issue of baptism. We ask those under 18 who wish to be baptised to check it out with their parents. If their parents are opposed to the baptism, then we request them to delay their baptism until the parents change their mind or, if not, until they reach the age of 18.

There is a principle that is correct: children, obey your parents.

What is written
'Honour your father and your mother' is a commandment written in the law of God and can be read in Deuteronomy 5:16. 'Honour' has the sense of 'respect' and gives to us the reminder that those who have long left their parental home

and are parents themselves should still respect their own parents. Jesus picked up this point in his teaching:

> *And he said to them: 'You have a fine way of setting aside the commands of God in order to observe your own traditions! For Moses said, "Honour your father and your mother" and, "anyone who curses his father and mother must be put to death." But you say that if a man says to his father or mother: "Whatever help you might otherwise have received from me is Corban" (that is, a gift devoted to God), then you no longer let him do anything for his father or mother. Thus you nullify the word of God by your tradition that you have handed down' (Mark 7:9–13).*

When a Jew declared something 'Corban', it was exclusively dedicated to God. A Jew could declare a sum of money, which was his, as Corban, in which case the money would have to go to the temple. At the same time, this man may have had parents in desperate financial need. Because of the vow of Corban, it would not now be possible for the man to help his parents, despite the command that they should be honoured. It is clear that Jesus is very unimpressed by following a religious practice that means that parents are dishonoured.

In the name of serving Christ, we could actually dishonour our parents. 'I'm so busy serving the Lord, that I don't have any time for my parents.' This would be a failure to respect our parents and would not be evidence of a Spirit-filled life.

It is even appropriate to consider the question as to whether we should put elderly parents into a Residential Care, or Nursing, Home. If in fact we are simply dumping a problem for us, then that can hardly be an honouring of our parents. But as a husband, say, I also have to consider the needs and pressures on the rest of the family. There is a balance to be considered here of how best to honour parents but also fulfil my responsibility to care best for my wife and my children.

Reward

In his quotation from Deuteronomy about honouring parents, Paul also recalls this is the first commandment with a promise attached to it – 'so that you may live long and that it may go well with you'. Actually it is not just the first commandment with a promise but the only commandment with a promise attached to it. Perhaps we should understand it as a primary commandment and that it carries a promise.

In the list of the Ten Commandments, this one comes after the commands about honouring God and before any of the commands telling us to honour our neighbour. Therefore we may be meant to see honouring our parents as a way that we can honour God. This is primary, before considering our neighbours, and it is a command that carries a promise. But it also presents us with a problem, because there are those who have honoured their parents, but have neither prospered nor had a long life.

We can make two comments. Firstly, the promise was originally given to the nation as a whole, so we can see this as a promise for society. A society will know a sense of stability, will prosper and even survive long term where there is good family life. All this is threatened when there is widespread disintegration of family relationships. Our politicians would do well to note this.

Secondly, we have to distinguish between an absolute promise and a general principle. With regard to family life, a favourite and often quoted verse is: 'Train a child in the way he should go, and when he is old he will not turn from it' (Proverbs 22:6). But this verse can be very painful for those parents who have given their children excellent training and then seen them turn wild. What we have here is surely a general principle. In general it is true that if parents train their children in the way that they should go, then they will keep to it. But we cannot say that an individual child will never wilfully choose to rebel.

So with the promise attached to honouring parents, we

may need to see it as a general principle rather than absolutely true in every single instance.

Parents to children

'Fathers, do not exasperate your children; instead, bring them up in the training and instruction of the Lord' (Ephesians 6:4). 'Fathers' here should probably be understood to include 'mothers' – so we are reading of the parents' responsibilities to their children. Similarly, in the same chapter of Ephesians and in verse 23, we read, 'Peace to the brothers ...' but the sisters are obviously meant to be included.

In practice, when it comes to parental behaviour, the father is more likely to exasperate his children through domination and the mother to do so through manipulation. The New English Bible translates verse 4 as: 'Do not goad your children to resentment.' I think of the stickers I have seen on large camper vans that read: 'We are spending our children's inheritance'!

Bearing in mind that a Roman father had the power of life and death over his children, the apostle is suggesting restraint rather than the harsh use of authority. Life in the Spirit leads to a different kind of parenting. There are principles of responsibility, training and instruction contained in this verse.

The rest of this chapter, Family, suggests some practical implementation of these principles. Behind these practical suggestions are not so much individual verses of the Bible but a mixture of experience, wide reading and conversations with other Christian parents.

Responsibility
'Bring them up' (v. 4). Parents have an awesome, but joyful responsibility to their children in that they are to bring them up. I agree with those who suggest that except where it cannot be avoided, children should not be sent to a boarding school.

Parents have a God-given responsibility to bring up their children.

Years ago my wife, who has no Christian heritage, had a strong conviction that, rather than look back, she should build forward and believe for a Christian dynasty. We felt our investment and prayers for our children were certainly answered when both our sons became Christians and then married Christian women. We see our sons' wives as answers to our prayers that we prayed years before we even knew them. Now with grandchildren, we feel a responsibility in prayer for the next generation.

There are important issues to consider in the bringing up of children
We must give attention to their age, for children need to be handled differently at different ages. In the early stages of a child's life, he or she is totally dependent on parents. Wise parents realise when to begin to let go, bit by bit, up until the day the child leaves home. Certainly, we can let go too quickly. Do we allow a 13-year-old daughter to decide how late she will come home at the weekend? We need to talk to other parents of teenage daughters on issues like this and not be dictated to by our child.

On the other hand, we must avoid a possessiveness that makes us always unwilling to let go. At the most extreme an adult child can be made to feel guilty about leaving home to get married. The Bible is clear; children leave the home of their parents to cleave to someone else. We need to bring them up confident to do that.

We should take care not to force our views onto our children. Children grow and begin to assert their own opinions and they have a right to do so. Sometimes their opinion is contrary to that of their parents. It is just possible that sometimes they are right! For parents to force their opinion upon a child often causes resentment.

It is so important not to force a decision for Christ upon a child. The decision is certainly a right one, but it is wrong for a parent to force it. It can be quite easy to do this when children are young and wanting to please their parents. But regeneration is a work of God's Spirit and to seek to force a decision will bring a crisis later on. Some children are converted when they are very young. Wise parents will observe what God is doing and go with that. The temptation though, is to force a decision, out of a natural anxiety to see your child saved. However, even that motivation can be false, for it can be based on the parents' desire to avoid grief and pain for themselves.

Parents should not expect a child to be more spiritual than they are. It is very easy for a father to neglect reading the Word himself and then become anguished that his teenage son has not opened his Bible for three months. No parents can impose a greater spirituality on their children than they have themselves. Parents need to model something through their own way of life.

Discipline
This is the training aspect that Paul mentions in verse 4: 'bring them up in the training and instruction of the Lord'. Today, we are not so much facing the question of what kind of discipline we should apply, but should we apply any discipline at all? A failure to bring correct discipline will not only result in unruly children but also in unruly parents. This is so noticeable in supermarkets today where you often hear disobedient children being screamed and shouted at by undisciplined parents.

In Hebrews 12 the writer speaks of God's children receiving God's discipline for their good. Reading between the lines we can see that discipline in family life indicates a true parent/child relationship. Discipline is for the child's good. It trains a child. Therefore just as God disciplines us for our good, we should discipline our children because we love them and want the best for them. Discipline must never be a matter of our venting our frustration.

Discipline needs to be moderate. Take the example of a son who has been warned not to play cricket too near a large window, then bowls straight through it. To tell the son he will never be allowed to play cricket again is immoderate and unrealistic. Discipline requires thought and self-control. Excessive discipline crushes a child's spirit.

Discipline needs to be consistent. This is especially the case when there is more than one child in the family. Children have a strong sense of what is fair.

Children should be allowed to present their case. As a pastor, I have had to learn from numerous examples where I have heard a side of the story from one person and been absolutely convinced that I have the whole truth, and that nobody else could persuade me otherwise. Then, I have heard the other side of the story from someone else only to find my former absolute convictions blown out of the window.

Parents must not jump to conclusions too quickly, but give a child an opportunity to explain. Obviously the child can be manipulative and the parents need to be discerning here.

Parents should always be hopeful. This is particularly true when children go through the teenage years and rapid physical changes and what my wife calls 'fizzy hormones' can make life at home somewhat tense. Inconsistency in teenagers is part of their growing up and discovering themselves. A teenager can be a rebel at home and vigorously arguing the case for Christianity at school. Wise parents will realise this and not despair during times of rebellion. I have seen so many rebellious teenagers become zealous followers of Jesus Christ. Parents need to keep patient and keep praying.

Instruction
Susannah Wesley, the mother of John and Charles, was also the mother of 17 other children. She must be one of the most formidable parents in all history. She gave individual time to each of her children each week and expected them to know the Greek alphabet, as well as the English one, while still very young. This may sound severe, but she trained up a son who helped to change the nation radically during a period of revival.

Parents instruct their children by example. A child with two parents should certainly know that Mum and Dad really love one another. Children should see their parents as lovers, not as quarrellers. Parents have an opportunity, through what they are together, to instruct their children and set a role model for a happy and secure marriage in the next generation.

An important time for instruction can be over a meal together. The practice of eating together around a table rather than eating around the television is well worth holding to. This should ideally happen at least once a day and certainly at the weekend. It can be an opportunity for direct instruction. As our sons were growing up, we read the Bible together or read an exciting Christian book at the end of the evening meal. Again, wise parents will judge when not to do that.

Special occasions can be very instructive. My wife once coined the expression 'happy family memory bank'. The idea was to seek deliberately to have occasions that would fuel happy memories in the years to come. Such happy joint memories help to hold a family together. I once read that orthodox Jewish parents seek to create such a climate of love within their family that their children will never want to leave the faith. That is a great challenge for Christian families.

To instruct our children, we need as opportunity arises to present a Christian viewpoint. Every day children are picking up other viewpoints from television, magazines, pop music and friends. Our children need to hear our voice, not by quoting chunks of Leviticus, but in presenting a Christian point of view where appropriate.

Never give up

In my church, we have members serving God with great passion who for years were far from God. Their parents kept praying for them.

One teenager, the son of a couple in my church, stopped attending about the first Sunday I arrived – you may not think that an odd coincidence! He was away from God for about twelve years during which time he married a non-Christian wife. The parents kept praying. The conversion of this young man's boss resulted in him and his wife coming on an Alpha Course. Today, he and his wife have major leadership roles within our church.

Parents, whatever age your children are, never give up.

Chapter 16   # Women
Equal but different

At the Dales Bible Week in 1978, Bob Mumford stated that the two major issues which would confront the church in the next few years would be the issue of authority and the role of women in the local church. It was definitely a prophetic statement!

The subject of women's role in the church is an issue of passionate debate, especially as we now have some of the New Churches recognising women elders and, of course, the Anglican church has to cope with strongly differing opinions on this issue, even though they now have women vicars. I do not believe I have all the answers on the subject; but I do want to attempt a serious contribution to the discussion.

The attitude that men hold on this issue is very important. Certainly, it must not be one of arrogance; women are to be honoured and respected in our churches. It is important also that we are not patronising in our attitudes. I realised one day how often people say to men in leadership: 'What do you allow the women to do in your church?' If we answer that question then we are almost bound to be patronising. I believe we should be affirming; 'This is how we encourage the women in our church.'

I have noticed three types of approach to this subject that I believe are unhelpful. Firstly, some try to laugh the subject away from debate. When I was teaching at a Bible College, we welcomed as a visiting speaker a well-known evangelical leader whose wife had recently preached a sermon at a major Christian celebration. He told the students that as he followed two men out of the meeting, one said, 'That was a good sermon'.

The other replied: 'It would have been better if preached by a man.' To which our visitor made the comment: 'As though the shape of a person's body makes any difference to the content of the message.' The students laughed heartily. Well, it may have been funny, but it did not actually deal with the issue – is it correct for a woman to teach a mixed congregation?

Secondly, some use emotion to attempt to manipulate a viewpoint on the issue. All of us have probably heard exhortations for men to repent because of their attitude towards women in the church. While not denying the vital need of repentance, we are only actually able to repent of sin committed. I am not convinced that the position that some men take on the role of women is necessarily sinful! I have heard women say: 'You don't understand how it feels to be a woman who can't stand up and preach what God has given.' Emotional statements like this must not be allowed to fudge a biblical examination of the issue.

Thirdly, some use their gift of oratory to address the subject. The result can be that a person is very persuasive about their viewpoint and yet not actually biblical. I remember hearing one very famous preacher passionately communicating the need to be thoroughly biblical on this subject as he spoke in favour of women pastors and elders. His oratory was very persuasive, but an objective listener could legitimately raise the question as to whether he, himself, was being thoroughly biblical.

In addressing this subject we need to be honest enough to recognise that some things are not crystal clear, and we must not be dogmatic in areas where there is a certain lack of clarity. At the same time we need to work through to some guidelines, rather than laying down none because everything seems so vague.

First of all what does the Bible actually say on this issue and what is a reasonable interpretation?

Then we have to consider our present cultural and social situation. Contrary to what is often said, Paul was not a man of his time with reference to women. Paul taught in his day that which would have been understood as the liberation of women. Today some can understand the same teaching as placing restrictions on women. Where we do see it to be right to place any limitations on the ministry of women, we need to be sure that these limitations are genuinely supported by the Bible, and also seek to understand the reasons for them. On a subject as sensitive as this, it is not good enough simply to close the argument with: 'It's in the Bible.'

Head covering

I see the passage in 1 Corinthians 11 as teaching us essentially about 'order' in the church, and it is therefore particularly crucial. We will pick up certain key verses.

Now I want you to realise that the head of every man is Christ, and the head of the woman is man, and the head of Christ is God (v. 3).

There are a couple of matters of crucial importance in this verse.

Firstly, the meaning of the word 'head'. The Greek word is *kephale* which is clearly used in two senses in this chapter. Sometimes it refers to the object on top of our shoulders, but at other times there is a metaphorical use of the term, as here in verse 3.

Some who teach a particular view of submission suggest that the metaphorical use of the word 'head' refers to 'source' (as in the head of a river), rather than one who has authority (as in headmaster). This runs us into all sorts of difficulties – not least here in verse 3 where, among other problems, we would have to see that the source of every woman is man. It seems to me that the reality is somewhat different; every man is actually born of a woman. So I believe we must see that the word 'head', when it is used metaphorically here, is referring to an authority or a leader. I heard the theologian Wayne Grudem state at a leaders' conference in Brighton that the greatest Greek expert in the world says this is the only way the word was ever used in classical Greek.

Secondly, this verse upholds the vital doctrine known by theologians as the 'Economy of the Trinity'. An understanding of this is essential to an appreciation of the Bible's whole teaching on submission. There is only one God, but in three Persons: God the Father, Son and Holy Spirit. The three Persons of the Trinity are co-equal and co-eternal, but the Trinity functions 'economically', so the Son submits to the Father, and the Spirit to the Father and Son. This is a voluntary submission that allows the work of salvation to be accomplished, but in this submission there is no lack of equality in essence within the Godhead. When in John 14:28 Jesus said: 'the Father is greater than I', he was not giving a proof text to Jehovah's Witnesses, but stating his voluntary submission to the Father while exercising his earthly ministry.

This pattern of equality with submission in the Godhead, helps us to see God's order for the relationship between husband and wife, and for the relationship between leaders and women in the church. In Genesis 1 we read that God created both male and female in his own image. And in Christ, there is absolute equality between men and women (Galatians 3:28), but for men and women to function 'economically' or efficiently there is a need for voluntary submission.

Mutual submission without leadership leads to a stalemate (see chapter 14, Marriage). But the headship of men over women, whether as a husband or as a church leader, does not imply inequality any more than the headship of God over Christ implies inequality within the Trinity.

And every woman who prays or prophesies with her head uncovered dishonours her head – it is just as though her head were shaved (1 Corinthians 11:5).

This raises a question. Why was the matter of head-covering an issue at Corinth anyway? To date, I have found only two reasonable possibilities, though there may well be others.

It may have been for a theological reason. The women in Corinth may have so grasped hold of their freedom in Christ that they felt it was no longer necessary to wear a covering to mark their moral virtue – if that is what it conveyed.

The other suggestion is that it may have been for a practical reason. It is proposed that the covering was actually a fairly comprehensive all-covering garment. So it may simply have been that wearing such a garment made it quite difficult to pray or prophesy in public. However, the removal of such a garment could be misunderstood to indicate moral looseness, which would then cause the woman to dishonour her head, probably to be understood metaphorically here as her husband. It would also bring dishonour on the church and, we can assume, on the woman herself as well.

Neither was man created for woman, but woman for man (v. 9).

In this verse we read that 'woman (is) for man'. This is a scripture that is clearly vulnerable to wrong interpretation by those who distort scripture 'to their own destruction' as Peter says. But the phrase needs to be understood within the wider context of scripture and it again provides us with a key to understanding godly order in the relationship of husband and wife. In Genesis 2:18 we read that woman is given to man as his companion; in that sense woman is for man. But Ephesians 5:23–29 teaches that the man's leadership and headship of the woman is to be expressed in his care for her. Such leadership and headship gives the woman a position of security and honour. 1 Corinthians 11:11–12 speaks of man's headship, but makes clear also men and women's interdependence.

For this reason, and because of the angels, the woman ought to have a sign of authority on her head (v. 10).

This is the most debated, and certainly the most crucial verse of this passage. There have been those who have interpreted it to mean that a woman ought to cover her head to show she is under man's authority. In this interpretation the covering is actually viewed as a sign of her submission.

There is another and, in the light of the above, I believe preferable interpretation; that the covering is actually a sign of the woman's authority. One commentator puts it like this: 'In Oriental lands the veil is the power, honour and dignity of the woman. With the veil on her head she can go anywhere in security and profound respect. She is not seen; it is the mark of thoroughly bad manners to observe a veiled woman in the street. She is alone. The rest of the people around her are non-existent to her as she is to them. She is supreme in the crowd ... But without the veil, the woman is a thing of nought, whom anyone may insult ... A woman's authority and dignity vanish along with the all-covering veil that she discards.'[1]

So in a church like the one in Corinth, the Christian woman would keep a covering on to show that she was in a position of security, dignity and respect from her husband and by the church (particularly important for single women). The covering actually served to underline her spiritual authority. To attend the meeting uncovered could indicate she was rebellious in spirit, disgracing her head, i.e. her husband and/or the church and its leadership and therefore not possessing the spiritual authority and dignity necessary for her to take part effectively in a meeting.

We must also consider the 'angels' mentioned in this verse. Some have compared this verse, unhelpfully I feel, with Genesis 6:1-2, where the 'sons of God' married the 'daughters of men'. That in itself is a very obscure passage, and probably does not help us here.

I would suggest a better comparison could be made with what Paul says about the church when writing to the Ephesians: 'His intent was that now, through the church, the manifold wisdom of God should be made known to the rulers and authorities in the heavenly realms' (3:10). It is reasonable to suggest that these rulers and authorities must at least include the angels, especially when we also compare 1 Peter 1:12 where, with regard to the gospel we read: 'Even angels long to look into these things.' If the angels of God observe the church and observe the church at worship – and that would remain true in every age and culture – and if God's wisdom is to be revealed through the church, how do these women with their heads covered affect the angels? Surely, it is as they see godly order in the church. By this we include men who lead in a righteous way, exercising their headship according to the biblical pattern, and women therefore in a place of security but ministering with dignity and spiritual authority.

The end of this passage contains two verses that are difficult to interpret because of some ambiguities.

For long hair is given to her (i.e. the woman) as a covering (v. 15).

More literally this should be translated: 'For long hair is given to her *instead* of a covering.' In practice, both translations could be used to serve the idea that long hair could be regarded as a woman's covering. That in itself leaves a certain ambiguity about the need for women (especially those with long hair) to cover their heads. In the New International Version footnote, an alternative translation suggests that the whole passage is about a woman's hair, not about a veil. I have checked many Bible commentaries and in none of them is that alternative even mentioned. Also it does not seem to be the most likely interpretation of the Greek – though clearly it is not impossible.

If anyone wants to be contentious about this, we have no other practice – nor do the churches of God (v. 16).

It is very difficult to know exactly what Paul is referring to here. In the end it is hard to get away from what seems to be the most natural way of interpreting the verse, that women covering their heads in worship was the common practice of the churches.

Today?

I want to suggest some relevant application of this for the church today. Firstly, 1 Corinthians 11 does contain some apparent ambiguities, as we have seen with verse 15. I have given a reasonable and reasoned interpretation of these verses – but dogmatism is out of place here. We ought not to insist on a practice in the church that is unclear or ambiguous in scripture.

Secondly, we must be aware of our present cultural situation. An uncovered head in Corinth in the first century AD may have indicated a woman of loose morals. This is not the case in 21st century Britain.

Thirdly, the principle here is all important. Is there godly order in our churches? Are the men and husbands exercising proper leadership as indicated by scripture – not domineering, but in the case of both husbands and elders laying down their lives for their wives and the flock of God? Are the women in a position of dignity and honour, and therefore able to minister in the meetings with real spiritual authority? If not, it won't be accomplished simply by a woman putting a scarf on her head.

Above all, I want to plead for the contemporary relevance of all this. With the ambiguities of covering and hair my interpretation may not be entirely accurate – whose is? But essentially this passage is about order in the church of God. With total equality in Christ, there should still be a godly order in the way that men and women function in the local church – an order that can be observed by the angels. We live in a world of increasing disorder; there should be something distinctively different – a godly order – in the church of Christ.

What about the men?

As a footnote to all this, I have sometimes been asked about the significance of a man not covering his head referred to in verse 4. Again there is a difficulty in interpretation because some commentators state that it is unlikely that the Jewish man used his tallith or veil as early as this. If the Jewish man did not pray with his head covered at this time anyway, and Paul speaks of man dishonouring his head if it is covered, that does produce some difficulties! So it is suggested that Paul possibly mentioned what would be wrong for a man so that he could make his real point about women.

But let us suppose that men were wearing the tallith at this point. Why? It was because of a misinterpretation of an event in Israel's history. They believed Moses veiled his face to hide the glory of God which shone on it. In 2 Corinthians 3:12,13. we see that Paul teaches that Moses veiled his face to hide a glory, which was in fact fading away.

The Jews copied the veiling but Paul argues in 2 Corinthians 3 that the veil has been taken away in Christ, the glory of his gospel being no fading glory, but rather, a lasting glory. Therefore a man covering his head dishonours his head (surely Christ being meant here), not recognising that the veil has been taken away in Christ. Indeed this could even be why the Corinthian women wanted their covering removed – they understood that in Christ the veil was removed. Therefore a man should not wear a covering for a *theological* reason – but a woman should wear a covering for a *cultural* reason; she was in danger of being regarded as a prostitute without the covering.

Women taking part in a meeting

It is clear that in the New Churches the women are encouraged to take part in the meetings. 1 Corinthians 11 speaks about women praying and prophesying and the context clearly seems to be that of public worship. We reject an interpretation of 1 Corinthians 14:34: 'women should remain silent in the churches' as having any reference to women making no vocal contribution to the meeting. This would immediately contradict the text just mentioned in 1 Corinthians 11 about women praying and prophesying – in the very same letter!

However, this does demand some interpretation of 1 Corinthians 14:34. In what sense are women to be silent in the church? There are several interpretations.

Firstly, that the women should not 'chatter' during the meetings. Those who reject this view, out of hand, seem to overlook what I call 'mobility' in meetings. It is very unlikely that in an early church meeting men and women would have sat together in a formal pew-type atmosphere. Whether or not the men and women sat together, it is likely that there was considerable coming and going to and from the meetings. So the women may well have been inclined to chatter on the fringes of the meeting, which was somewhat disorderly.

Secondly, that the women should not 'weigh' prophecy. The plain fact is that such an interpretation strains the passage – it seems nowhere near the natural and common sense interpretation that hermeneutical principles demand.

Thirdly, that the women should not ask questions at the meeting. This could refer to either questioning the teacher at a public meeting, if the teaching was given in a dialogue kind of way, or it could refer to the woman asking questions of her husband concerning the teaching – after all the women are instructed in this passage to ask questions of their husbands at home.

Whatever the precise interpretation, the prohibition would seem to be along the lines of women not creating disturbances in public meetings by chattering and/or asking questions. Certainly one would not expect a woman to be publicly weighing prophecy either, for reasons that will be seen as we look at 1 Timothy 2:12. What we can be clear about here is that there is not a prohibition on women contributing to the meeting in prayer, prophecy or with other vocal contributions that we shall touch on later.

The teaching issue

We come now to the vexed question of women teaching in a meeting. Paul writes:

> *A woman should learn in quietness and full submission. I do not permit a woman to teach or to have authority over a man; she must be silent. For Adam was formed first, then Eve. And Adam was not the one deceived; it was the woman who was deceived and became a sinner (1 Timothy 2:11–14).*

This is the passage, which more than any other, raises the question as to whether a woman should preach to a mixed congregation. However, the situation again is not without some ambiguity. Acts 18:26 describes Apollos being instructed in their home by both Priscilla and Aquila (Priscilla is mentioned first!). Titus 2 states that older women are to teach younger women 'what is good'.

There is also one verse regularly overlooked in this discussion about women teaching: 1 Corinthians 14:26 – 'When you come together, everyone has a hymn or a word of instruction ...' (literally 'teaching'). Now exhorting everyone, as we do from this verse, to bring something to the meeting – be they male or female – we must face the fact that 1 Corinthians 14:26 would lead us, if we are consistent, to exhort the women, as well as the men, to bring teaching, as well as other contributions mentioned in the verse.

Returning to the Timothy passage, the exegesis is certainly not straightforward. It also suffers from the many attempts these days to make it appear as though it says it *is* permissible for a woman to teach in the church before a mixed congregation. In the face of difficult exegetical hurdles, we can be tempted either to give way completely and say: 'Oh, let the women teach and be elders; it is the twenty-first century after all.' Or we can take the opposite view and simply dig our heels in dogmatically and say: 'Ignore the complications; verse 12 says that women are not allowed to teach and that's it.'

Now there are those who argue very strongly from the viewpoint of cultural relativity and use the example of slavery to support their case. The force of this does need some serious consideration. The New Testament does not teach the abolition of slavery and in the context of the times we understand why – it would have been a suicidal doctrine to encourage slaves to try to seize their freedom. Slave rebellions were always put down with savage force by Rome. But all would agree that the seed for the abolition of slavery is sown in the New Testament, and that such abolition, spurred on by men like Wilberforce, was a thoroughly Christian act appropriate to a later time and a different culture.

That the New Testament teaches the emancipation of women is undeniable. So the argument goes, that what would have been culturally entirely unacceptable at that time, i.e. women teaching and having authority over men, is thoroughly acceptable and even biblical in a later time and a different culture. After all, Britain has had a woman Prime Minister, which shows how much things have changed. This point can be responsibly argued and is more than simply saying, because it's happening in the world, let it happen in the church.

But does cultural change mean we can ignore the original teaching of this passage? It has been helpfully pointed out that while we tend to emphasise the prohibition of verse 12: 'I do not permit a woman to teach or have authority over a man ... ', the real emphasis of the passage is actually in the permission of verse 11: 'A woman should learn in quietness and full submission.' The impact of that needs to be appreciated in a time, society and culture that often considered women unworthy of being taught!

What of the reason for the prohibition on women teaching in verse 12, which is given in verses 13–14: 'For Adam was formed first, then Eve. And Adam was not the one deceived; it was the woman who was deceived and became a sinner'? The point of difference between Adam and Eve is that Eve was deceived by the serpent into eating the fruit while not knowing the command of God given before her creation that the fruit was not to be eaten. Adam deliberately broke the known command of God when he ate. But, is it really better to be taught by a man who knowingly breaks the command of God, than by a woman who is deceived when not knowing the command?

Some believe that Paul is teaching that women are more vulnerable to deception, and that could be regarded as deeply offensive, but the real issue is whether or not it is true and a right interpretation of scripture.

A preferable interpretation would seem to recognise that this again touches on the whole matter of headship. I would say 'preferable' because when faced with a really difficult verse or passage of scripture to interpret, it is best to try and see it within the wider context of scripture. While not convinced that there is a biblical doctrine of women's proneness to deception, I am convinced of a biblical doctrine of headship.

Adam's headship is demonstrated in the order of creation. Adam was formed first, then Eve (v. 13). Eve's sin was a demonstration of a failure to observe God's order – she took the lead. But we need to bear in mind that the Bible charges Adam, not Eve, with introducing sin into the world (Romans 5:12ff) and therefore the principle of headship and responsibility is kept firmly with the man.

One point that makes the exegesis of the 1 Timothy 2 passage more controversial is the unique use here in the New Testament of the Greek word *authentein* – 'to have authority'. It has been suggested that in classical Greek the word was used to describe authority in sexual matters. Therefore it is proposed that it is on this subject that women are prohibited from teaching men; it is not a general prohibition of their teaching of men. Again one cannot help feeling that this strains the natural sense of the passage.

How then do we deal with the prohibition? It is vital to appreciate the whole thrust of scripture as well as the immediate context. Whatever the exegetical difficulties of these verses, do we not have to bear in mind the matters of headship referred to in 1 Corinthians 11 and the whole teaching on male/female relationships in Ephesians 5?

My argument is this – that where the Bible would restrain a woman from a teaching ministry it is not to create difficulties, but it is to act with mercy. In other words, women in the church are not to be put in a position where they carry an ultimate responsibility in matters of exercising authority.

Neither are they made vulnerable to criticism by giving the public teaching of doctrine. Rather the men are called to take the lead in carrying the weight of these burdens and the women are to be cared for, secure and honoured, so they can minister with spiritual authority within the church. Some may want to dismiss this as simply old-fashioned, but the Bible is actually teaching a different order from that which so often we find in the world.

Recognising that any approach to this matter is open to the possibility of strong emotional reactions, frustrated hopes, arguments over exegesis and concern for cultural relevance, we still have to take courage and set guidelines in the light of all the above.

Firstly, it would mean that women do not teach mixed congregations in our churches. In practice, in our church, this means a woman does not preach at our Sunday services. However some take the view that it is possible for a woman to teach a mixed congregation as long as she does so under the oversight of the elders who therefore carry the final authority.

Secondly, the women are encouraged to take the fullest possible part in our meetings. This could include a brief and spontaneous 'teaching' contribution as part of the general flow of charismatic worship. Also there would seem to be no reason why a woman should not lead worship as long as an elder is present. This is to ensure that should a difficulty arise in worship, which requires authority to be exercised, the man takes the responsibility and not the woman.

The role of women in ministry

There seems to be little doubt, as far as the New Testament is concerned, that women could be deacons. 1 Timothy 3:11 may well refer to female deacons rather than the wives of deacons. We also read of a female deacon named Phoebe in Romans 16:1. The Greek will not allow the translation 'deaconess' as though this could be some kind of separate species. 'Deaconess' is only valid as a translation if it is understood to refer to a female deacon.

When we ask what a deacon did in New Testament times, we actually possess very little information, even from the Bible itself. The word deacon does of course mean 'servant' and the apostles often referred to their own ministry with this term. No one can truly minister in the church, be they apostle, elder or whatever, without also being a deacon, or servant, of the church.

I do not believe that men or women were appointed deacons as such, but there were those who by virtue of their ministry could be referred to as deacons. Such ministries could be many and various, but would involve taking the lead in some serving ministry within the church. Such deacons were not invested with eldership authority. Now this leadership might be exercised in intercessory prayer, administration, or caring for the needy. Some of these ministries might be such as women particularly excel in, without wanting to suggest that these ministries are innately feminine.

1 Timothy 5 speaks about a list of widows. It would appear from this passage that those listed served the church in some way, having proved their character by their conduct in the life of the Christian community. They were presumably supported financially by the church. We certainly know from early church history that this became the case in practice. To bring this up to date there may be single women and widows in our churches who have a lot to offer in terms of ministry, who at present are not being properly recognised and used.

One wonders about Philip's four daughters who all prophesied (Acts 21:9). The reference is tantalising, but while it does not demand us to believe that these gifted women were travelling prophets, it does surely require us to believe that they did rather more than offer the occasional blessed thought in a worship service. The women clearly had a ministry and, while I would not want to argue too much from that one reference, it was a ministry that at least demanded recognition.

I quote David Pawson from another context than this passage, but it is immediately relevant: '... there seems to be a distinction between the human authority inherent in an 'office' of leadership and the divine authority of a revelation whoever communicates it. To pass on a message from God ... is not seen as exercising leadership authority.'[2]

We must not overlook Luke's reference to the women who ministered to Jesus and the disciples (Luke 8:2,3). There is also the reference in Romans 16:7 to Junias (usually a female name) who was 'outstanding among the apostles'. The brevity of the reference forbids us to build this into a doctrine and may mean she was outstanding in serving the Apostles. But even if Junias was only (!!) the wife of Andronicus, she is obviously worthy of a mention. Indeed both of these references indicate that Jesus' larger team and New Testament teams included women.

Again how do we make all of this practically relevant for today?

Firstly, women are not recognised as elders within many of the New Churches. Not only is there no positive reference to this in scripture, but also we have seen reasons for this with regard to the whole matter of headship. It is important however to remember the contribution of the elder's wife. It would seem appropriate at times to ask the viewpoint of an elder's wife on an area of church life, without making her responsible for any decision that follows. An elder's wife may have a distinctive ministry of her own, or her role may be that of vital support to her husband's ministry.

Secondly, when a ministry team travels, we should expect that there would be women in such a team. They have much to bring to a team in terms of prophecy, prayer, counselling of enquirers etc.

Thirdly, women as well as men should be recognised as deacons within the churches. Responsibilities could be diverse, but must demonstrate a leadership within their area of deaconing. A woman deacon could be full-time in her ministry.

Fourthly, other women could serve in the church full-time, even without the need to recognise them as deacons. This would approximate to the role of widows in the New Testament in 1 Timothy 5.

Clearly, verses such as Galatians 3:28 and 1 Peter 3:7, teach the essential equality of men and women in Christ. But I believe that we must also remain consistent in that we teach the biblical doctrine of headship and submission. We therefore see certain functional differences in the church between men and women. It is important to encourage women in their ministry and, where we do place limitations, to know why we do.

Notes
1. *1 Corinthians*, A. Robertson and A. Plummer, The International Critical Commentary, T&T Clark, 1967, pp. 232–233.
2. *Leadership is Male*, J. David Pawson, Highland Books, 1988, p. 28.

Chapter 17   Kingdom
The expression of God's will

I had been living in Brighton about a year and was waiting at the station to catch a train to London. I suddenly realised that my old college Principal, now retired and also living in Brighton, was waiting for the same train. Travelling together for the next hour inevitably meant a great deal of nostalgic talk about college life. Resisting the temptation to challenge his marking system with respect to my essays many years earlier I did introduce the subject of the kingdom of God, which I remembered had been a favourite lecture theme of his.

I observed that at that time I had not really appreciated the importance of this subject, but now realised how dominant it was in the Bible and how relevant it is for the way we build the church and understand Christian discipleship. For him, listening to this was probably a bit like the experience that preachers sometimes have of constantly teaching on a particular subject in a local church only to find that the same subject, when briefly touched on by a visiting speaker, is greeted by the congregation as some incredible new and life-changing revelation. However, my old Principal was gracious enough simply to acknowledge that we sometimes need a different context to really understand something that we may have heard many times before.

There is no question that among the New Church movements of the 20th and 21st centuries the theme of the kingdom of God has been a real provocation. It would be difficult to conceive of a church being restored to a thoroughly biblical pattern without some clear understanding of the nature of God's kingdom. As John Bright says: 'the concept of the kingdom of God involves, in a real sense, the total message of the Bible.'[1]

Old Testament background

Although the kingdom of God was central to Christ's teaching, it does have a substantial Old Testament background. For example we read in Psalm 145:10–13:

> All you have made will praise you, O Lord; your saints will extol you. They will tell of the glory of your kingdom and speak of your might, so that all men may know of your mighty acts and the glorious splendour of your kingdom. Your kingdom is an everlasting kingdom, and your dominion endures through all generations.

However, the pinnacle of Jewish hope regarding God's kingdom is expressed in the book of Daniel:

> In the time of those kings, the God of heaven will set up a kingdom that will never be destroyed, nor will it be left to another people. It will crush all those kingdoms and bring them to an end, but it will itself endure for ever (2:44).

Such scriptures as these gave rise to hopes of God's intervention for the nation of Israel and the prospect of defeating every enemy, followed by an elevated and prosperous position for Israel.

Therefore, when Jesus came preaching about the kingdom of God he was not really introducing a new idea, but rather reawakening hopes that had always been there in the nation. The shock value of this statement by Jesus, then, cannot be overstated, when he said: 'Therefore I tell you that the kingdom of God will be taken away from you and given to a people who will produce its fruit' (Matthew 21:43). The very people who had expected to be part of this kingdom are now being threatened with dispossession.

During the 400 years of prophetic silence, from Malachi to John the Baptist, the rabbis had taught the people to expect the breaking in of the kingdom. They had taught that the voice of the prophet would again be heard and that God would bring salvation to Israel. The Jews, now under Roman oppression, heard that a wild man was out in the desert proclaiming: 'The kingdom of God is at hand.' No wonder the crowds flocked to listen to this new prophet, John the Baptist.

Then, as Jesus comes on the scene and the first words he speaks in Mark's gospel are: 'The kingdom of God is near' it is hardly surprising that he causes a stir. John Bright observes: 'For all his repeated mention of the kingdom of God Jesus never once paused to define it. Nor did any hearer ever interrupt him to ask, "Master, what do these words 'kingdom of God' which you use so often mean?" On the contrary, Jesus used the term as if assured that it would be understood and indeed it was. The kingdom of God lay within the vocabulary of every Jew. It was something they understood and longed for desperately.'[2]

What is the kingdom of God?

It is important not to view the theme of the kingdom of God as some vague theological concept. Rather, it was being eagerly awaited by Israel and it was the burden of Jesus' own ministry.

Both in the Hebrew and Greek languages the word 'kingdom' has the sense of an authority and sovereignty exercised by a king. It is this note of authority that is important to understand, because the word 'kingdom' is not highly significant for people who live in what is called the United Kingdom. In fact Britain has not been a true kingdom for centuries, but functions much more like a republic.

In Britain there is a Head of State and a Head of Government. The Queen reigns, but the Prime Minister rules. There are only ten things that the Queen can do by her own authority. When we realise that these include such an unlikely event as having the casting vote if there is a dead heat in a General Election, we can see that these ten responsibilities do not add up to much! The citizens of Great Britain are not really subject to the Queen, but to the Prime Minister who, with his or her party, rules.

In a kingdom, one man rules. His will is the law. There is no room for debate, opposition or voting. His position is usually inherited and so are the people he rules over. By such a definition the United Kingdom is not a kingdom. But when we talk of the kingdom of God we are acknowledging that God *reigns and rules*. So the kingdom of God speaks of the real rule and authority of God; it speaks of God's government. I personally tend to define the kingdom of God as *God's will being expressed*.

The kingdom has past, present and future expressions.

The kingdom of God has come
John the Baptist spoke of the nearness of the kingdom, but pointed to the arrival of Jesus on the scene. Jesus began his ministry by declaring, 'The kingdom of God is near ...' Mark 1:15). There can be no doubt as we study the gospels that the kingdom was inextricably linked with the person of Jesus himself.

If the kingdom of God is God's will being expressed then that is exactly what Jesus did. 'For I have come down from heaven not to do my will but to do the will of him who sent me' (John 6:38).

To Peter he says: 'I will give you the keys of the kingdom of heaven ...' (Matthew 16:19). We can note here that commentators agree that Matthew nearly always used the phrase 'kingdom of heaven' to avoid using the name of 'God' when writing his gospel, primarily for Jewish readers, who could have been sensitive about this.

Jesus also identifies himself with the kingdom when he talks about the kingdom of God being 'within' or 'among' people (Luke 17:21). The inference is clear; the kingdom is among people because Jesus is among them.

Then, again, Jesus does the works of the kingdom. In Luke 4 we read of Jesus going into the synagogue in Nazareth and reading from the scroll of Isaiah. The passage he read was in effect the manifesto of the kingdom. It describes what God's government looks like. This is why the congregation gave him their close attention. We can imagine them thinking, 'What is Jesus going to say about this scripture?' Jesus did not disappoint them by being anything less than radical. He said: 'Today this scripture is fulfilled in your hearing.' Indeed it was, for from then on Jesus began to preach the good news and heal the blind and release those who were oppressed, just as the prophet Isaiah had said.

The very clearest identification of Jesus personally with the kingdom probably comes in what he says in Matthew 12.28. 'But if I drive out demons by the Spirit of God, then the kingdom of God has come upon you.'

It has been said that what we call the ministry of Jesus is the rule of God. In Jesus we see God's will being expressed.

The kingdom of God now
The kingdom of God finds an expression right now through the church. The kingdom is not confined to the church, because the church cannot claim a monopoly on the whole rule of God. Nevertheless if the kingdom is about God's will being expressed, there should be some demonstration of that through the church. So in the church we should be able to see evidences of the government of God in miracles, healing, release of the oppressed and the overthrow of evil.

There will always be limitations in the present age when it comes to doing the works of the kingdom. Indeed there were limitations even in what Jesus did. He did the works that expressed God's will, but it was always in a finite expression of them. So, he healed the sick, but at some point those same people would have become sick again. He raised Lazarus from the dead, but Lazarus at some point died again. I have been to two tombs of Lazarus; one is in Bethany where Lazarus is supposed to have been buried the first time. But there is also a tomb in Cyprus where it is claimed that Lazarus was buried a second time after serving as bishop of that island. Whether or not either tomb is authentic, the existence of both makes the point that Lazarus died twice.

Jesus stilled a storm on Galilee, showing God's rule over nature, but there have been plenty of other storms there since then. Against this background we can understand why in John's gospel the mighty works of Jesus are referred to as signs. A sign points to something. The works that Jesus did, point to the future coming of the kingdom in all its fullness when there will be no more sickness, no more death and God's government will be exercised in perfect peace.

So in the church we expect to see the signs of the kingdom, for if God's will is not expressed in and through the church then is the church really being the church? However, this side of Christ's return we are not going to see the will of God perfectly expressed; there will always be limitations.

The kingdom to come
When we pray, 'Your kingdom come', we are obviously looking to the future breaking in of the kingdom in its fullness. This will happen when Jesus returns at the end of world history. We have already seen in chapter 1 that it will be a day of restoration. There will be new heavens and a new earth, a consistent theme in the Bible's teaching.

The fullness of the kingdom will also be expressed in an undisturbed perfection. God says: 'I am making everything new!' (Revelation 21:5). And specifically he mentions that there will be no more death, or mourning, or crying, or pain. All those signs that Jesus did, pointing to the fullness of the kingdom, and all those signs seen in the present age through the church, will be perfectly demonstrated in the age to come.

And Jesus will be King, which will be clear for all to see. Jesus is Lord right now, but that fact is not recognised by millions of men and women. When Jesus returns, and brings in his perfect rule forever, then it will be obvious to everyone. 'Then the end will come, when he hands over the kingdom to God the Father after he has destroyed all dominion, authority and power. For he must reign until he has put all his enemies under his feet' (1 Corinthians 15:24,25). This King will pick off every enemy, even death will be destroyed – the kingdom will come in its fullest expression.

So, we can look back and see that Christ was establishing the kingdom through his ministry. The signs of God's rule were always in evidence when Jesus was on the scene. We should see something of the kingdom right now demonstrated through the church. We see it as the gospel is preached with power and the people of God do works of the kingdom. But we still look forward to the kingdom to come when there will be a new creation. There will be no more suffering or death or sadness, but we shall enjoy the fullness of God's presence. God's rule will be perfectly manifest forever.

Bringing in the kingdom

Paul writes to the church at Rome:

> I will not venture to speak of anything except what Christ has accomplished through me in leading the Gentiles to obey God by what I have said and done – by the power of signs and miracles, through the power of the Spirit. So from Jerusalem all the way round to Illyricum, I have fully proclaimed the gospel of Christ (Romans 15:18–19).

Bearing in mind that Jesus spoke of the gospel of the kingdom going to all the nations, what Paul says here definitely helps us to understand the nature of that gospel. In the past some have seen the gospel as something to be proclaimed only in words, viewing actions as a social gospel and miracles as a counterfeit gospel. Paul gives us a much broader perspective here.

Words

We need to proclaim the gospel in words. 'How, then, can they call on the one they have not believed in? And how can they believe in the one of whom they have not heard? And how can they hear without someone preaching to them?' (Romans 10:14). The importance of communication in words, even though preaching is so often criticised today, is seen in annual political conferences when speech after speech is given to the delegates to win hearts and minds.

But for preachers of the gospel more than just skill with words is required. 'For we know, brothers loved by God, that he has chosen you, because our gospel came to you not simply with words, but also with power, with the Holy Spirit and with deep conviction' (1 Thessalonians 1:4,5). So the gospel does come with words, but not just with words, there is a need for the anointing of the Holy Spirit. I often feel this when I read some of the sermons preached during a time of revival. Judged by the words alone, those messages were not always very remarkable, but the effects were remarkable. This goes to show the absolute need of the Holy Spirit to anoint the preaching.

'So then, just as you received Christ Jesus as Lord, continue to live in him' (Colossians 2:6). The only way we can receive Jesus is as our Lord as well as our Saviour. We cannot receive Jesus as Saviour at conversion and then later make him our Lord. He is Lord and he must be proclaimed as making a change of government in a person's life when we receive him.

Works

God looks for justice and compassion for the poor.

> *He does not oppress anyone, but returns what he took in pledge for a loan. He does not commit robbery, but gives his food to the hungry and provides clothing for the naked. He does not lend at usury or take excessive interest. He withholds his hand from doing wrong and judges fairly between man and man ... That man is righteous (Ezekiel 18:7-9).*

Helping to meet the needs of the poor is one way of extending the rule of God on the earth. Not all believers are gifted for street evangelism or to be preachers, but some do have a gift of mercy that can be used to reach the poor.

At one of the Newfrontiers Leadership Conferences a key message was preached from Paul's exhortation to 'Remember the poor'. Adding to some firm convictions already in place concerning the kingdom of God, this message helped to launch a whole new wave of initiatives among the poor across many nations of the world. Large offerings have been raised, not usually to fund direct feeding programmes, except in situations of extreme emergency, but to help many who are poor and unemployed to help themselves.

This is not just some token social action because it seems like a good idea. It is very much seen as part of the outworking of the gospel of the kingdom. God's rule is to be extended on the earth at the present time. When the kingdom comes in its fullness there will be no more sickness, or poverty or hunger. To preach the gospel of the kingdom includes dealing with these issues as best we can now. However, if all that we do in the future is centred on ministering to the needs of the poor we will have become just a welfare agency and have failed to be the church. But if we only preach the gospel in words then it will fail to be the gospel of the kingdom.

Wonders

I have seen large crowds turn up for evangelistic meetings where the people have certainly not come for the preaching, but they have come to see some wonders. An Indian evangelist, Ram Babu, visits our church each year. He can fill our large church building, not primarily because of his preaching, but because of the amazingly accurate words of knowledge that he brings and his effectiveness in praying for the sick. Again, this is in line with proclaiming the gospel of the kingdom. The New Testament records this as the method used by Jesus. 'This salvation, which was first announced by the Lord, was confirmed to us by those who heard him. God also testified to it by signs, wonders and various miracles, and gifts of the Holy Spirit distributed according to his will' (Hebrews 2:3,4).

Reading the story of Jesus' ministry in the gospels, we see on a number of occasions that the crowds were attracted to Jesus by what he did rather than by what he said. 'Now the crowd that was with him when he called Lazarus from the tomb and raised him from the dead continued to spread the word. Many people, because they had heard that he had given this miraculous sign, went out to meet him' (John 12:17–18). However he then took the opportunity to preach to them. (See also Mark 3:7,8). Jesus performed signs and wonders to call attention to the preaching of the gospel; the challenge is there for the church today.

Kingdom lifestyle

There are only two verses in the New Testament that actually define the kingdom of God. Both begin with a negative before going on to the positive. 'For the kingdom of God is not a matter of eating and drinking, but of righteousness, peace and joy in the Holy Spirit' (Romans 14:17). In context the negative part of this verse means that the government of God is not expressed in rules and regulations, but it is expressed positively in righteousness, peace and joy.

Maybe charismatic Christians have particularly warmed to the theme of the kingdom, because this righteousness, peace and joy are in the Holy Spirit. Everything we do should express these positive qualities as a mark of the Spirit-filled life and as a contribution to bringing in the rule of God.

Let's take the example of money. Money needs to be handled righteously. We can easily be tempted to cheat with money. We can cheat by filling in our Tax Form incorrectly or by failing to renew our vehicle licence. But this does not express the will of God and so does not advance the kingdom.

We should also be at peace with money, which would

certainly make a good contrast with the attitude of so many in the world. 'Keep your lives free from the love of money and be content with what you have, because God has said, "Never will I leave you; never will I forsake you"' (Hebrews 13:5).

If we love money, then striving will replace peace. If we are anxious about money, then contentment can easily turn to jealousy. But God has promised that he will never leave us or forsake us and he says that in the context of money. Responding to this promise of God, the writer continues, 'So we say with confidence, "The Lord is my helper; I will not be afraid. What can man do to me?"' (Hebrews 13:6). Well, man can send us a large gas bill, but we are to live confidently and at peace, for the Lord has promised to be our helper. This is kingdom lifestyle.

Righteousness has to do with the way that we use money. Peace has to do with our attitude to money, but joy has to do with the way that we give money. In 2 Corinthians 9:7 Paul tells us to give our money joyfully – even hilariously, to make a very literal translation of the Greek. To take on tithing as a duty and then to give our money through gritted teeth does not represent a kingdom lifestyle. As people of the Spirit we demonstrate the rule of God in our lives when we give our money joyfully.

Power

One other verse defines the kingdom of God: 'For the kingdom of God is not a matter of talk but of power' (1 Corinthians 4:20). Most believers know that the Greek word *dunamis* is the word we translate as 'power' here. It's the word from which we get our English word, 'dynamite'. Preachers often like to play on this term and talk of God's kingdom being explosive like dynamite. But that is incorrect for the simple reason that when Paul wrote his letter to Corinth, dynamite had not been invented!

Originally the word had the meaning of power to

transform something. For Christians there is always the temptation to talk about the need for things to change. But that is not kingdom lifestyle. Rather we express the will of God when we start affecting and transforming life in our society or community. In my own church we have a ministry to the homeless on the streets of Brighton and have purchased and staff a home where we can genuinely help such people. We are seeing their lives transformed and that is the *dunamis* that is spoken of here. We can talk with no power. The kingdom of God is the power to see things changed.

The church is involved in extending the rule of God across the earth. It is an ever-extending kingdom and at some point all the nations of the world will feel its impact. However there will always be limitations and Jesus reminded us that we would always have the poor with us. But we always look for the return of the King. Then the rule of God will be fully established forever.

Lord, may your kingdom come, may your will be done, here on the earth as it is in heaven. One day it will be.

Notes
1. *The Kingdom of God*, John Bright, Abingdon Press, 1988, p. 7.
2. *The Kingdom of God*, John Bright, Abingdon Press, 1988, pp. 17–18.

Chapter 18   # Mission
Making the difference

In July 2003 the Newfrontiers family of churches hosted a leadership conference in the Brighton Conference Centre. Looking back to this, in a few years time, it will almost certainly be viewed as a watershed event. It was, of course, a gathering of leaders, the great majority of whom were pastors. But what marked out this conference in a particular way was the call to mission that came through so persistently. This call had been heard in Newfrontiers conferences before and, indeed, there was already a stirring to plant new churches across the nation and the nations, but this conference was tangibly different. It was as though reaching all the nations was now the overwhelming priority.

Why is mission such a priority?

It is easy enough to say we commit to mission in order to see people saved. This is absolutely true, but it can be such a familiar idea that the motivation is not strongly there to support that conviction.

There are several statements made in Romans 15 that bring the theme to us in a way that helps to stir our passion in this area:

> *For I tell you that Christ has become a servant of the Jews on behalf of God's truth, to confirm the promises made to the patriarchs so that the Gentiles may glorify God for his mercy, as it is written: 'Therefore I will praise you among the Gentiles, I will sing hymns to your name' (vv. 8, 9).*

To follow through a vision for mission for taking the gospel of the kingdom to the ends of the earth means that we are going to see more worshippers of Jesus. The Bible certainly teaches that God's people will come under pressure and that there will be persecution, and indeed, martyrs for Christ. But the idea that the church will simply be reduced to a tiny remnant and then Jesus will return just in time to stage a rescue before she is squeezed out all together, is certainly not a biblical one.

When we live in the one continent in the world where the church is not growing, it is too easy to feel we are simply set on an irreversible slide of decline. In reality we belong to a global movement that is winning tens of thousands of new people every day who will forever be worshippers of Jesus. Every day that history continues we can be certain that there are not yet enough worshippers of Jesus and that there will be more. More Gentiles will yet glorify God for his mercy as Paul tells us in Romans 15.

'And again, Isaiah says, "The Root of Jesse will spring up, one who will arise to rule over the nations; the Gentiles will hope in him"' (v. 12). As we commit to mission it will mean that there will be so many more into whose lives hope will come and who will add to the number of those praising Jesus on the earth, and who will continue to worship him forever in heaven. Indeed immediately after speaking of the Gentiles coming to hope in Christ, Paul goes on in verse 13 to speak of overflowing hope. This is not a vague hope that things may get better, but in the New Testament hope is eschatological and is both sure and certain.

Paul speaks to Titus of 'a faith and knowledge resting on the hope of eternal life' (Titus 1:2), and again of the fact that 'we wait for the blessed hope – the glorious appearing of our great God and Saviour, Jesus Christ' (Titus 2:13). So we hope for eternal life and the return of the Lord, both of which hopes will unite as Jesus comes again to usher in the eternal age.

When I have led a thanksgiving service for a believer who has died, I have always used words at the time of the burial which state: 'We commit our brother's body to the ground and his soul to the Lord, in sure and certain hope of the resurrection to eternal life.' The hope is not vague, it is an absolute and certain hope. We live in a world in which many people increasingly fear what will happen in the future. In recent years there has been a huge upsurge in the number of terrorist outrages around the world and our politicians speak of the certainty of more to come. It is easy enough to fear the worst today and then to worry about the future. To be involved in a mission to the ends of the earth will be to see people's fear replaced with a sure and certain hope.

Where is our confidence?

One of the most motivating statements to world mission must be the words of Jesus in Matthew 24. 'And this gospel of the kingdom will be preached in the whole world as a testimony to all nations, and then the end will come' (v. 14). It is often pointed out that the phrase 'all nations' will bear the sense of 'all people groups'. Not only is this an appropriate interpretation of the Greek terms, but it also brings clarity. Nations as we see them today have often been artificially constructed and designated. Nowhere is this more evident than on the African continent where straight-line national boundaries remind us of somewhat arbitrary decisions made by previous colonial powers for where national borders should be drawn.

But within a particular nation there may be several people groups. In India the number probably approaches 500 such groups distinguished by such factors as language, culture and a self-awareness of their own peoplehood. Our confidence for world mission is firmly tied to this promise of Jesus that all people groups will hear the gospel of the kingdom before the end comes.

A rather superficial approach to this might suggest a couple of radio broadcasts to a people group, or dropping in some evangelistic tracts that might therefore do the job. However, the Scriptures would definitely indicate rather more than this. In Revelation 5 we read: 'And they sang a new song: "You are worthy to take the scroll and to open its seals, because you were slain, and with your blood you purchased men for God from every tribe and language and people and nation"' (v. 9). So now we see our confidence for world mission is not only the statement by Jesus that the gospel will reach all people groups before the end of history, but that the blood of Jesus has been shed to purchase people for God from all such groups. This requires more than an evangelistic blitz on a particular people group, but rather the establishment of a church. If the sacrifice of Christ is sufficient actually to purchase believers from each group there must be a church established in each group. Our confidence, therefore, is that each of the world's peoples will have a worshipping community of believers.

Even this is further emphasised in Revelation 7:9,10:

After this I looked and there before me was a great multitude that no-one could count, from every nation, tribe, people and language, standing before the throne and in front of the Lamb. They were wearing white robes and were holding palm branches in their hands. And they cried out in a loud voice, 'Salvation belongs to our God, who sits on the throne, and to the Lamb.'

So here John, the author of the Book of Revelation, is given a vision of what actually happens in the future – there will be those from all peoples who, for all eternity, will worship Jesus.

So our confidence for world mission is the promise of Jesus, the effectiveness of the blood of Jesus, and a forward look at a great multitude of worshippers of Jesus. If we commit to mission then we will be seeing more of the multitudes drawn from all peoples who will become those with an eschatological hope and who will adore and praise the Lamb of God.

What is the method?

Our method in mission is unashamedly to plant churches.

I have a friend in Bangalore, India, who leads a vibrant, growing church and is himself very gifted in counselling and in deliverance ministry. A few years ago a large crusade was held in the city, led by a well-known evangelist. My friend was asked to head up all the counselling and follow-up teams.

Each night the gospel was preached to crowds of up to 40,000 people and many apparently responded to the message. Yet, despite my friend's premier position in the follow-up, not one convert was added to his church through the crusade and apparently this was typical across the churches in the city.

My purpose is not to criticise the evangelist, who is a great communicator of the gospel with an extraordinary passion and zeal to make Christ known. Indeed his preaching of the gospel there in Bangalore may well have broken up the ground and made it easier for others to bring the gospel to individuals in the weeks and months following. However, we know it to be true that, despite some individual exceptions, the enormous cost and organisation of such vast crusades do not lead to many being directly added to local churches.

A much more effective method of evangelism in seeing people both saved and added is through the planting of local churches. Now it is possible to plant churches and, by doing so, do no more than move the furniture around. A group can go from one local church, be planted in another town, attract a few disaffected Christians from other established churches, and by that means see some growth. However, that adds nothing to the kingdom of God overall and can hardly be thought of as a meaningful advance for the church.

But when a church is planted with a vision in its heart to reach the town or city where it is established, and then when individuals are converted, and baptised, and when these new Christians join that new planting, then the church is on the move. Again and again it has been found that church planting is the most effective way to break into a new area. This is not a hit-and-run strategy. The family of God is really and visibly present; it begins to extend God's rule into the community; the fruit of the evangelism is contained.

Church buildings

When we talk of planting local churches we are definitely not talking of buying or building premises. We are not talking of church buildings. I belong to a church where we have had to do some serious thinking and then some even more serious re-thinking about buildings.

When our church was originally established in 1978 with a group of about 70 believers there was such excitement with regard to new charismatic life, apostolic ministry, a new freedom in worship and small groups meeting in homes that the whole idea of a church building seemed a non-issue. Our church was meeting in a hired school hall when even the need to bring your own chair added to the sense of an exciting new pioneering adventure.

We were quite vocal in those days about not having a permanent building and not putting large financial resources in that direction. As it happened, we were given a 400-seat building, which was at risk of becoming redundant due to its very small, and reducing, congregation. We then spent some hundreds of thousands of pounds to make it fully useful, including the removal of dry rot and repairing other evidences of advanced decay!

But in general, the cost of buildings, and the fixed pews that have so often produced rigid formality in a typical church building, had been enough to put us off. However, that has to be weighed against the growth in the size of a congregation that then begins to produce all kinds of different pressures. For us to cope with 1000 people in a hired hall every week would obviously not be impossible, but it certainly would not be easy. Having therefore outgrown our first building we were eventually to spend £3.6 million on a new facility.

Had we changed our minds about buildings? In principle, no, but yes, we were now seeing the value of a permanent facility to help us as a base for our mission. We have carefully avoided references to our building as a church, because it is not a church. Our church name is Church of Christ the King and we meet on Sundays in a building that we call the Clarendon Centre.

Although years ago we would never have dreamed of spending so much money on a building, this in itself has had some unexpected benefits. Right through the time we were raising the £3.6 million that we needed, we gave away ten per cent of all the money that came in. We also found that, in the period in which a building fund was open, there was an extraordinary release of generous giving in the church and that has continued in the years following the completion of the building. This has enabled us as a church to give away hundreds of thousands of pounds every year to evangelism, church planting and social action.

Today, some are suggesting that the church ought to return to the New Testament pattern of meeting only in homes. Along with this there tends to be the further suggestion that such House Churches should only reach a maximum of about fifteen people.

It is true that in the New Testament period the church probably did meet almost exclusively in houses. At that time other buildings would not usually have been available to the church community. Paul, of course, was able to use a lecture hall in Ephesus for two years of evangelistic ministry.

I remember once looking round the ruins of a Roman villa in Paphos in Cyprus, a town where Paul himself ministered. As I looked at the area of the main hallway in the house I calculated that if Christians had owned this villa and then hosted church meetings there, it could certainly have accommodated at least a hundred people.

If we go to the other extreme and suggest that a church cannot meet in a house we are again in danger of making the church dependent on our particular view of a building. In some countries, certainly in many Muslim countries, the church meeting in a home may be the only viable option. The point is that we must plant churches and not church buildings. The merits of any building have to be considered simply on the basis of how it helps the church in her mission.

Spiritual warfare

Jesus said: 'I will build my church, and the gates of Hades will not overcome it' (Matthew 16:18). This was actually a declaration of war. Jesus was making clear that Satan would have to back off and give up on claims for people for his kingdom, for the church will advance and gather people into a redeemed community. The devil has been fighting back ever since that declaration by Jesus. Spiritual warfare therefore becomes most intense in the building of the local church.

Paul reminds us in Ephesians 6 that the devil has schemes (v. 11) and that we have to face days of evil (v. 13). The schemes that Satan has are aimed at destroying the local church and the days of evil are times of especially severe attack by Satan against individual believers or against a whole church community.

I have noticed that Satan has different schemes for new church plantings and for established churches.

With a new church planting, Satan's desire is to kill it off as soon as it starts. Almost always we find that those moving to establish a new planting have huge difficulty in selling their house. Very often there has been a lot of sickness among those trying to establish the new work. Satan does not want it even to start.

When a church has been established, Satan will try to wreck the community by stirring up irreconcilable divisions between members. These divisions are not really ones that cannot be healed up, indeed looking at them objectively the issues often seem simple and easy to resolve. But there are demonic powers that can make the simplest difficulties become suddenly complicated and apparently impossible to resolve.

Watch out for the devil's schemes.

Vision for mission

If the church does not have a vision for mission, then the church is not restored to the biblical pattern. The gospel will be preached to every people group before the end comes. Every nation will have a church. There will be more worshippers of Jesus than there are today, those who will yet move from despair to hope. To fulfil this vision we must plant churches. The blood of Jesus, as well as his promise, guarantees our success in this mission, though not without a battle. A glimpse into eternity in the Book of Revelation confirms that the mission will be completed.

Over the years I have met a few men who seem to be living with the conviction that if it is only up to them they will, together with the stream of churches they work with, get the gospel out to every people group. Ted Haggard of New Life Church, Colorado Springs and Dr Joseph C. Wongsak of Bangkok in Thailand seem particularly motivated in this way. The more individuals and the greater the number of churches that develop a similar conviction, the quicker the job will be done and Jesus will return.

The New Churches are churches on a mission, that together with other parts of the body of Christ on earth, they will preach the gospel of the kingdom to all nations, plant churches in all people groups and see the rule of God extended to the ends of the earth.

Chapter 19   # Flexibility
Living in harmony

I have always enjoyed the story about the young student from a training college who went to visit a church that was showing some interest in asking him to be their pastor. During the visit the young man was introduced to the senior deacon, who had held office for some forty years. 'Young man,' he said, 'I've been a deacon during the time that seven different pastors have served this church.' The hopeful next pastor replied, 'You must have seen a lot of changes in that time.' 'Yes,' replied the deacon, 'And I've resisted every one of them.'

By contrast to this, some years ago I was talking to an Anglican vicar who was beginning to see a number of members join his church after leaving one of the New Churches. I was interested in his point of view on this. 'I think,' he said, 'that some people get weary of living with constant revolution.'

So on the one hand it can appear that what we tend to call the traditional churches are stuck in their ways, refusing ever to change and taking on the appearance of an extinct dinosaur. On the other hand we have the New Churches, which can appear a whirl of constant change.

It is true that some of the New Churches have, at least informally, adopted a motto of 'constant change is here to stay'. There have been new church plantings unable to obtain a secure meeting venue in the early days that have moved around like a nomadic people and therefore given the impression that they are never settled.

While resisting the idea that it is good to have change simply for the sake of change, it would be true to say that the New

Churches have generally been prepared to be flexible and not to resist change, and that this has been a strength. At one time all new church movements have had to be innovative.

John Wesley preached in the open air and formed his converts into societies or home groups to share their experiences of the faith. The early Baptists broke rank with the established church and baptised believers by full immersion. William Booth trained his converts like an army, dressed them in uniforms and had them play musical instruments on the streets.

Sadly, what begins as radical and new can sometimes settle to become traditional and unchangeable. So the challenge for the New Churches it to retain their flexibility without simply jumping on every new bandwagon. To quote John Piper preaching his first sermon in a series based on the Letter to the Romans, 'I am not as moved now as I used to be by the tyranny of the urgent and by the need to respond to every trendy view that blows across the cultural sea in America. Well past midlife, I have a deep confidence that the best way to be lastingly relevant is to stand on rock-solid, durable old truths, rather than jumping from one pragmatic bandwagon to another.' The point is well taken.

The Newfrontiers group of churches is one of the New Church streams that has certainly shown great flexibility. It is the stream to which I belong, and I am going to give a number of examples. I am sure that these are not the only possible examples, but they serve as a reminder of the need to keep open to change.

Head coverings

In the early days of what are today being called Restoration Churches or New Churches there was probably an over-correction to what some had previously experienced in other churches. Some had experienced situations where men seemed to be weak in church leadership and women seemed to be very strong. It was felt that there needed to be a much more manly approach evident among the church's leaders.

But more than this, it was felt that there should be a proper understanding of what was meant by 'headship' and that this should be worked through, not only in the church but also in marriage and family life as well. It was against that background that it was seen right for women to wear a head covering during the meetings to symbolise a fresh understanding of headship and submission.

Frankly, it probably helped to make a healthy statement in the early days, but a more enlightened biblical perspective began to break in. I have tried to outline this in chapter 16. There was enough flexibility to abandon head coverings when it was realised that, though we had rediscovered a vital biblical principle about headship, it was not best expressed today by the women wearing scarves on their heads.

Buildings

Again, I touched on this matter in chapter 17. In the early days of the New Church movement there was a protest against investing in permanent buildings, in order to keep us flexible. Permanent buildings with fixed pews were seen as inhibiting a new-found freedom in worship and wasteful of money which could be better invested in ministry. However, in the course of time, it began to be seen that with growing congregations a building could be a useful base to facilitate the ministry of the church. A permanent building also helps to convey the message that this church is serious about staying in the neighbourhood; it's not packing up tomorrow and disappearing. We were flexible enough to change our thinking here, but need always to keep alert to the fact that a building is to help us with our mission and must never become the goal of our mission.

Small groups

The New Churches have always seen the value of small groups and this is something that has become almost universal throughout the whole body of Christ. The challenge has been to understand what shape of small group is the right one at any particular time. Again we have been very flexible here. Sometimes such groups have really existed simply to assist relationships and friendships in the church. Sometimes the groups have been more task oriented, involved in some ministry together; for example serving the homeless in a town or city.

More recently many of the churches work with what are often called 'cell groups' which try to combine both the building of community and outreach into the neighbourhood. Sometimes groups have been formed on the basis of geography, sometimes on the basis of common interest. Sometimes leaders have sought to direct people into a particular group; sometimes it has been a totally free choice. None of the churches feel that they have to adopt a particular small group system or even any small group system. It is an area where we remain flexible.

Other voices

I once led a church where during one period I preached every Sunday morning and evening for thirteen weeks before I allowed anyone else to speak from the pulpit. In retrospect I admire the persistence of the congregation that was prepared to live with such a lack of variety! As a family of new churches we have tried to keep very open to other voices that are not from our particular church stream, and indeed are never likely to be. We have recognised that God raises up men in all sorts of different situations who can helpfully speak to us.

Years ago John Wimber, from the Vineyard Group of churches, brought us into a much fuller understanding of the kingdom of God and the ministry of healing.

The Baptist preacher and theologian, John Piper, has helped us enormously to keep appreciating the greatness of God and the joy of following him. He spoke at one of our own conferences in Brighton.

Dr. Joseph C. Wongsak was responsible in his ministry to us for creating a new expectation for church growth and church planting. His own vision was to plant a church in each of more than 600 districts in his home nation of Thailand by the year 2000. He did it ahead of schedule and certainly inspired us.

C. J. Mahaney, who oversees a group of churches known as Sovereign Grace Ministries, has repeatedly thrilled us with his magnificent preaching and helped raise our expectations of how the preaching of Reformed doctrine in a charismatic setting can really set the hearts of God's people on fire.

There would be many other examples, but these different voices serve to show that we have kept flexible, listening to those from other streams. None of us has a monopoly on the truth.

Moves of God

There was a heated controversy over what was often termed 'The Toronto Blessing' towards the end of the 20th century. It was controversial in that many in the church saw it as a fresh move of God and others did not see it as a move of God at all. What happened during 1994 and 1995 particularly was that many believers were testifying to a fresh encounter with God and the results of those encounters were often highly visible. People fell on the floor, waves of laughter swept across congregations. Some people jumped around, others shook violently.

When people do unusual things, especially in a church meeting, there are bound to be some criticisms. On the whole the New Churches accepted what took place as a genuine move of God, although, as on all such occasions, it was recognised that sometimes the flesh got in the way of the Spirit.

It has been suggested that it was not really an authentic

move of God because there was no lasting fruit. But that can be questioned. Apart from individuals who would still testify to how God met with them afresh at that time, there are two long-lasting results in the churches. Ever since 1994 there has been a lot more expectation in what we now call 'ministry times'. It has become very common to invite people forward for prayer and ministry at the end of a meeting. This has become a much more normal part of church life.

Again, ever since that time there has been a much greater evangelistic thrust from our churches. What in '94 and '95 was often referred to as the River of God did not become a moat; it has flowed out into our communities.

Church planting

This is another area in which we have had to remain very flexible. The New Churches have always believed that this is the best way to evangelise the nations, but we have had to adapt.

Early on, the method used was usually to send a fair-sized group to a new area, ideally 30 to 50 people, and immediately put in a full-time leader. This is an extremely expensive method of church planting and therefore tended to limit the number of new works. Also, those volunteering to be part of a new church plant like this were sometimes carrying their own agendas, especially desires for leadership positions that had never come their way in the church they had left. If such hopes were again not realised it sometimes led to some frustrations with the new church. It has not been unusual for a church planted in this way quickly to lose all its original members.

Generally, a more flexible approach is now used. A group of people begin meeting in a home and, as the numbers grow, other home groups can be formed until it is believed that there is enough of a critical mass to come together, usually on a Sunday morning, and establish a permanent church presence. Often leadership simply arises through the ranks, although sometimes a full-time leader will then be called in from elsewhere.

A few years back, at Stoneleigh Bible Week, a stirring prophetic word challenged the Newfrontiers group of churches to believe for 1000 churches in the UK. Again, we have been flexible enough to start developing strategy for the number of new church plants that will be required. Will we reach the number of a thousand churches? Well, we are certainly having a really good try.

Stoneleigh Bible Week

The Bible Week run by Newfrontiers for ten years up to 2001 was a success by any reckoning. In the final years well over 20,000 people were attending and in fact there had to be a repeat week to cope with the crowds. There were powerful times of meeting with God in the worship, and much stirring and prophetic preaching from the main platform. Over the years hundreds of seminars gave instruction on everything from *Home Schooling* to the *End Times* and from *Handling your Money* to *Enriching your Marriage*. There were magnificent programmes for children and teenagers. And it was a lot of fun as individual churches camped together for a week and enjoyed great fellowship with thousands of other Christians.

Now it is difficult enough in the Christian church to close down something that is failing. Stoneleigh Bible Week was closed down when it was a success. Why? There was the flexibility to see that the time for gathering was over and the time for going had come. Now, instead of a Bible Week once a year there are dozens of outreach events that take place across the country. To close down a Bible Week that was so successful could be regarded as crazy, but we have sought to remain flexible and respond to the voice of God.

The future

A challenge that faces the New Churches is to remain flexible. We can look back and see how willing to embrace change we

have been. But will we always be like that? There is the possibility of creeping paralysis. In the years to come we might seek
to analyse where we have been willing to change, only to find
that gradually we resisted it and started to settle. Paul warns
us in Galatians 3:3: 'Are you so foolish? After beginning with
the Spirit, are you now trying to attain your goal by human
effort?'

There are undoubtedly many areas where the New
Churches will need to change in the future. I see three in
particular.

Cell groups

In many churches cell group structures have been introduced
which are the result of studying the teaching of Ralph
Neighbour on this subject[1] and the model has often been some
of the huge cell churches in Asia. I suspect that unless we
remain flexible in this area, cells in many churches will wither
and die.

Even as I write, we are hearing of some churches adopting
what is called the G.12 model or again the Freemarket cell
model. I will not seek to describe these for this is not a book
about cells and the models may themselves be overtaken by
others in the years to come. But there are big challenges to face
with any cell structure.

Work demands for many people today are so great that a
cell meeting at 7.30 p.m. on a Wednesday evening is just not a
realistic possibility for many church members. Issues of
whether a cell structure really helps to disciple people, build
relationships and keep the church looking outward, need to be
constantly monitored.

As long as cells really serve the vision of the church, all
well and good, although even then we need to review whether
some adaptation is needed to keep them effective. Maybe, for
some churches at some stage, cells of any kind will not be the
most helpful structure. We need to remain open to change.

Sunday meetings

Sunday is not the Sabbath. A Saturday is the Sabbath, and is observed by religious Jews as it is enshrined within their Law. For the Christian there is a very good reason to meet with others on a Sunday, for every week there is the opportunity to remind ourselves that on this day Jesus rose from the dead. However, even here I see that it will be necessary to keep flexible.

I often travel to teach in Dubai, one of the Emirates of the United Arab Emirates. The churches I visit there have their main meetings on a Friday because this is a Muslim country and the day when most people, including most Christians, are not working. To have been inflexible on this point and insisted on only meeting on a Sunday would have severely limited the opportunities for the churches there to advance.

But even in the UK I sense we are going to need to keep flexible about this issue. Shops are now open on a Sunday and more Christians have to work on a Sunday. It is possible, at least for some churches, that in the future Sunday morning, or even Sunday at any time may not be the best time to meet.

In my own church we decided at one stage to hold repeat meetings on a Sunday morning. We held a first meeting at 9 a.m. and the second meeting at 11 a.m. It just did not work; so we did not simply keep going with it; we changed. We then moved to a morning and evening repeat meeting on a Sunday and this has worked well. But it is possible that in the future it could be better still to meet, say, on a Friday evening and a Sunday evening. It is important that we do not simply settle where we are. We need to keep flexible. We may have to change again.

Leadership structures

In Acts 6 the apostles found themselves facing a problem. The early church was giving food aid to a number of widows who had joined the church. Those who came from a Greek background reckoned that they were being overlooked compared with those who came from a Hebrew background. What should the apostles do? They did not really want to spend a lot of time sorting out this issue when they understood that their priorities were in the areas of teaching and prayer.

So they consulted the church constitution, saw that a church ought properly to have seven deacons and made sure they got some responsible men from the church elected!

No! In reality of course the response was much more fluid. The apostles did not want to be pulled away from the main call of God upon their lives. So they decided that the best way forward was to ask seven men whose lives gave real evidence of faith and the Spirit to oversee the food aid distribution. It was simply a pragmatic and flexible response to a situation that arose.

Now the New Testament clearly teaches that there are elders and deacons in the church. However, the issue is not whether we have a certain number of elders or whether we have deacons to look after the practical needs of the church. Our approach will need to remain flexible. What leadership team does the church need at this stage of its growth? We will need to keep pragmatic, dynamic and flexible if we are going to have the right leadership structure at any particular time in a church's development.

Remaining flexible

We cannot turn to a particular verse of the Bible that commands us to be flexible. But we do believe that God speaks to us through his word and also through prophecy. If the New Churches are going to avoid institutionalism, traditionalism and even fossilisation there must be a continuing willingness to change as God speaks and leads.

Note
1. *Where Do We Go From Here?* Ralph W. Neighbour, Jr, Touch Publications, Inc, 1990.

Chapter 20 Hope
The King is on the throne

What hope is there for the future of the local church?

The world does not see much hope for the church, and the church does not see much hope for the world. At least that is how it often appears. The church in Britain is reckoned by many to be in terminal decline with members leaving at the rate of hundreds a week across the nation. Obviously, commentators use different sets of statistics to make their analysis and projections, but I have certainly read that the churches in England have lost a third of their membership in the last 30 years of the 20th century, and the prediction is that in another 30 years time church attendance in the UK will be down to two per cent of the population. Some suggest an even more severe decline than that, although others are more hopeful in stating that we may be at the bottom of the curve just before the statistics start to show a move upwards.

Certainly, in my own city of Brighton there are frequent discussions about closing down a number of the city's Anglican church buildings. This is somewhat in contrast to Tesco and Sainsbury's who are constantly constructing new stores or extending old ones.

Some see these trends as an indication of the new religious inclinations of our nation. People prefer to shop on a Sunday rather than go to church. The supermarkets are booming, which is very evident as you drive past their car parks after a Sunday morning meeting. Shopping malls seem to have become the new centres for worship as thousands gaze upon and adore the fashions and electronic gadgets as well as the jewellery and the DVDs.

I sometimes wonder whether the number of watches currently for sale in any town or city actually exceeds the total size of the population of that town or city. When I travel by plane I always check through the number of watch advertisements in the in-flight magazine. I have counted up to as many as 20 full-page advertisements for watches in some of them. What, I wonder, is this obsession today with the great god, watch!

A different story

But of course decline is by no means the whole story about the church in this nation. There are some churches that are seeing dramatic growth in the size of their congregations. During a period of study leave, that gave me the opportunity to visit four London churches, I attended packed services that in each case was only one of several that day, to cope with the large crowds attending the meetings. These four churches, as well as others in London, are now numbering their Sunday attendances in thousands rather than in hundreds.

While we can read books and magazines that are telling us of the need to break right away from anything like the Sunday gatherings that have previously been a focal and vital point of church life, there are churches who continue to meet with passionate expressions of worship and anointed preaching that are seeing huge growth in their numbers.

Not every church is going to be a Kensington Temple or a Willow Creek, probably because for one thing they do not have a Colin Dye or Bill Hybels as their Senior Pastor. However there really is no reason why every local church should not hope for growth and advance. Jesus has said he will build his church and there are multitudes of non-believers all around us. Therefore it must be possible to see new churches planted and it must be possible to see established churches grow.

The new church movements are committed to that and

they are seeing it happen. They are working to biblical principles that are outlined in this book, and seeing genuine
advances in planting and growth. It is true that these advances
may not be happening as quickly as many would like to see, but
there is a forward momentum. The New Churches are generally full of hope for the future and no plans are being made for
a funeral.

In Isaiah 62 God says: 'For Zion's sake I will not keep
silent, for Jerusalem's sake I will not remain quiet, till her
righteousness shines out like the dawn, her salvation like a
blazing torch' (v. 1). It is important to see this verse, and
indeed this whole chapter, in its original context. Isaiah was
prophesying to a people facing exile and the destruction of
their nation. But whatever devastation the people would have
to go through, they could live with the promise that God's eye
was upon them, and that his passion was for Jerusalem; to see
the city restored as a shining light to the nations.

Now if Israel and Jerusalem of the Old Testament is all
that we see in this chapter, then what is written there could be
viewed as largely irrelevant to our situation today. In fact, it is
possible to see in a prophetic chapter like this not only something of a promise for that time, but also a promise for subsequent and later fulfilments. This is not a fanciful idea,
especially when we see that in the New Testament, the city of
Jerusalem becomes a title for the church. For example, 'But
you have come to Mount Zion, to the heavenly Jerusalem, the
city of the living God' (Hebrews 12:22). Again: 'I saw the Holy
City, the new Jerusalem, coming down out of heaven from God,
prepared as a bride beautifully dressed for her husband'
(Revelation 21:2). The picture of Jerusalem dressed as a bride
makes no sense unless it refers to the church.

So we can see that this scripture in Isaiah, speaking of the
restoring of Jerusalem, stands as a promise and hope of
restoration whenever God's people have been reduced to a low
state.

What particularly caught my attention years ago and

certainly enthused me with new hope for the church was the last verse of the chapter: 'They will be called the Holy People, the Redeemed of the Lord; and you will be called Sought After, the City No Longer Deserted' (Isaiah 62:12). The picture that so many people have today of the church is that she is deserted. They see crumbling buildings, small congregations, faded notice boards and conclude that the day for the church is over.

Added to this is the publicity that the church so often gets through the media, which hardly helps. There seems to be endless prominence given to rifts caused by differing views on gay issues, and the more controversial debates, such as the desire of some bishops to ordain gay clergy, get highlighted. In the public perception the church can be frankly pathetic.

But here at the end of Isaiah 62 there is the promise that the people of God will be sought after and seen as a city that is no longer deserted. In some measure the new church movements of the last 20 to 30 years would have some testimony to this happening. With the promise of God to restore his people's fortunes when they seem to have hit rock bottom there is hope for much more restoration and growth in the future.

Right attitudes

The New Churches have had to learn not to be triumphalistic in their outlook. Whenever there is a new start there is the danger of being like this because of the excitement engendered by novelty.

In the early days of the New Churches, with their initial very quick growth and huge Bible Weeks, it was easy to adopt an attitude that the churches would continue to grow at an accelerating rate to huge size and to do so very quickly. I remember 'words' that spoke of churches of twenties becoming churches of hundreds and churches of hundreds becoming churches of thousands. Frankly, it has not commonly, or hardly ever, been like that, although there has been steady advance.

I have known new churches to be planted with the initial

claim that they would be a refuge for many Christians who had been hurt and damaged in the past. After a few years these same people are claiming to have been hurt and misunderstood in the new church as well! I am simply acknowledging that when we build churches we build with people. People are unpredictable and churches can face intense pressures and spiritual forces of evil.

It is not easy to build a local church and it is a huge battle to maintain a local church. There are very real disappointments and individual failures. The New Churches are not immune to this and even if they began with a rather triumphalistic attitude, experience has tended to sober them.

At the worst we have to avoid giving way to cynicism about the church. There really is a battle on to plant, establish and grow a local church. But at the same time we have all the promises of God. If we will build in God's way, and we have the Bible to teach us that way as well as the Holy Spirit to lead and give us the power, then there is real hope of progress. The battle is real, but the hope is real.

Hope for the world

Hope for the church does in fact mean that there is hope for the world. At one level the church is a witness and demonstration that God is at work in the world. He is calling out a people from all the peoples to be his people. There is the good news of salvation being proclaimed by the church and the government of God is reaching the nations through the agency of the church. The church is able to give the answers to the really big questions of life. How did we get here? What are we doing here? Where are we going from here?

When there is an attempt to answer these questions outside the church, it can be a pretty depressing experience. We are told that we all began with soup. There was originally(!) a chemical soup that through a combination of sunlight and chance interaction of different elements produced a living cell from which life, as we know it, began. It has taken hundreds of millions of years and a slow evolutionary process, but what began as soup has now brought us the whole animal kingdom and the world population of over five billion human beings.

As to why we are here, one philosopher put it: 'The reason that we are here is to discover the reason that we are here!' Finally, we are going nowhere. We are mortal creatures and whether our lives are long or short we will end up as dust and with no consciousness. Paul puts it with stark simplicity and penetrating accuracy when he writes: 'If the dead are not raised, "Let us eat and drink for tomorrow we die"' (1 Corinthians 15:32).

The church brings to the world answers on these issues that are full of hope. We are on this earth by the will of God who has created the heavens and the earth. He also created man out of nothing as unique among all his created works. Only men and women have a revelation and understanding of God, only they can think about eternity and can be worshippers. God knows us; we are not here by a freak accident of evolution.

We also know why we are here. Three times in Ephesians chapter 1 the apostle tells us that we are to live to the praise of God's glory. We are here to bring pleasure to Jesus Christ. Properly understood that makes a difference to every moment of our life. Even in times of pressure and tragedy we can live to please the Lord. So what can seem to be the dullest, the most routine and the most difficult parts of our lives can be transformed by the knowledge that we live to please Jesus.

And as for where we are going, then this life at its fullest and most exciting and most stimulating only gives us a hint and a suggestion of the joy and wonder of glory to come.

Supremely, through its message of salvation, but also through its mercy ministries and its work into countless communities, the church is bringing hope to the world.

Different views

As we consider the issue of hope we do have to recognise that Christians have sometimes taken extreme and opposite views with regard to the future. Some see a future where everything in the world simply gets worse and worse, the church is persecuted and nearly extinguished, but just before it is too late Jesus returns to rescue his remnant people.

The doctrine of the 'remnant' is one that is certainly there in the Bible, but has been picked up by some people who want to impose it upon the whole church. We can see this theme being taken up in the Letter to the Romans where we read: 'So too, at the present time there is a remnant chosen by grace' (11:5). In context, Paul is talking of the way that in Elijah's time, despite the widespread apostasy of the nation, there still remained 7000, a remnant, who were faithful to the Lord and had not bowed the knee to Baal. Paul goes on to make the point that in his day there was a small number, a remnant, of the Jewish people who had acknowledged Jesus as Messiah and Lord. That is still true today; I live in a city where there is a strong Jewish community. Out of that community there is a small number, a remnant, who are followers of Jesus Christ. But it is a very big, and I would suggest unjustifiable, jump from that to suggesting that a remnant is all that Jesus will have when he comes again.

On the other hand, or at the other extreme, there is the view that everything will get better and better for the church and as a result for the world as well, so that eventually most of the world's population will turn to Christ. Only then will Jesus return. This is known in Christian theology as post-millennialism and interprets the thousand years of Revelation 20 as being symbolic of a long golden age in church history when most of the peoples of the earth become converted.

Rather than a remnant people this is a picture of a glorious church made up of most of the world's population. To support this viewpoint a scripture such as the one in Romans 11 that speaks of the full number of the Gentiles coming in is used. But, again, this is a big jump. Not only does this view leap from a statement about the full number of the Gentiles to meaning the majority of the Gentiles, it also jumps right over verses that suggest pressure and setbacks for the church in the End Times. Jesus specifically says: 'Because of the increase of wickedness, the love of most will grow cold, but he who stands firm to the end will be saved' (Matthew 24:12,13).

A positive viewpoint

It can be very tempting simply to go for a position that is comfortably halfway between these two extremes. In reality it becomes impossible to speculate about the numbers or percentages of people that will finally be saved. What is clear is that an unstoppable work of God goes on in good times and bad times, and even in times of great hostility and persecution. History demonstrates to us that in such times the church is often strengthened, although many people also fall away.

The early Christian writer, Tertullian, famously commented: 'the blood of martyrs is seed,' usually quoted as: 'the blood of the martyrs is the seed of the church.' This reflects what was happening at the time. There were many people who became Christians because they saw the bravery and witness of the martyrs for Christ. At the same time there were even some bishops who denied their faith in order to save themselves from being put to death. Persecution has always tended to produce these different results within the church.

What we can say for certain is that every people group will hear the gospel and there will be those redeemed from every people group who will worship before the throne of the Lamb (Matthew 24:14; Revelation 7:9). The number that will finally stand before the throne will obviously be huge because the reference in Revelation speaks of a great multitude that no-one could count. However both in Matthew and Revelation these references to the evident triumph of the gospel are read among other references to persecution and martyrdom.

It seems right therefore to expect as we draw closer to the end that the darkness of the world will grow ever darker, which will be in contrast to the light of the church that will grow ever brighter. Arthur Wallis wrote '... the growing darkness will only make the light shining from God's people seem all the brighter. God will conclude this age as he commenced it. Great power and glory in the church, great victories over Satan, but in the context of great persecution and opposition.'[1] So the planting of churches and the ingathering of vast numbers of believers takes place at the same time as persecution increases and nominal Christians fall away. Also there will be genuine believers who will lose their lives because of their testimony to Jesus, but whose witness will greatly encourage others.

Revival?

Some believers talk of a great end-time world revival. But this is difficult to prove from the scriptures themselves. In the history of the Christian church there have been many revivals, most of which have been relatively short-lived and usually geographically limited.

For example the 1904 Revival in Wales lasted for about two years, though obviously its effects lived on for many years. Until Jesus comes again there is every possibility that such revivals will continue to occur. In Western Europe we could argue that we are good candidates for a revival, considering the low state of the church as a whole.

Much as we may hope for revival, our hope is not in revival. Our confidence must be in the fact that Jesus has promised to build his church, and to do so in every nation. So, revival or no revival, there is plenty for God's people to do from today until the end of history and to do so with the absolute hope of success.

We live in a world where everything is shaking or will be

shaken. Believers belong to the kingdom of God that will stand amidst the shakings. And when everything has been shaken to the point of collapse the one thing that will remain will be the church of Jesus Christ.

Because the church is what Jesus is building, because the church is the body of Christ on the earth, then the church will be offering hope to the world until the day the King returns.

Note

1. *Rain From Heaven; Revival in Scripture and History*, Arthur Wallis, Hodder and Stoughton, 1979, p. 124.